T0196484

# Jocelyn's Journey

By Elizabeth Jones

Edited by Eric Monson

WESTBOW
PRESS®
A DIVISION OF THOMAS NELSON
& ZONDERVAN

Scripture quotations are from the ESV® Bible (The Holy Bible, English Standard Version®), copyright © 2001 by Crossway, a publishing ministry of Good News Publishers. Used by permission. All rights reserved.

WestBow Press books may be ordered through booksellers or by contacting:

WestBow Press
A Division of Thomas Nelson & Zondervan
1663 Liberty Drive
Bloomington, IN 47403
www.westbowpress.com
1 (866) 928-1240

Because of the dynamic nature of the Internet, any web addresses or links contained in this book may have changed since publication and may no longer be valid. The views expressed in this work are solely those of the author and do not necessarily reflect the views of the publisher, and the publisher hereby disclaims any responsibility for them.

Any people depicted in stock imagery provided by Thinkstock are models, and such images are being used for illustrative purposes only. Certain stock imagery © Thinkstock.

ISBN: 978-1-5127-6570-0 (sc)
ISBN: 978-1-5127-6571-7 (hc)
ISBN: 978-1-5127-6569-4 (e)

Library of Congress Control Number: 2016920113

Print information available on the last page.

WestBow Press rev. date: 11/30/2016

"It is time for breakthrough," he continued. "For healing beyond your expectations. You are going to dream and I need you to write it down. Write a book. Don't worry about the critics. Don't deny or hide the testimony I have given you. It is for God's glory. What the enemy has intended for bad, will be used to bless others. There will be healing beyond your expectations. He is rebuilding everything, worry not and be ready!"

# Acknowledgements

To my dear friend, Eric Monson, without you, I would have never finished this project. Thank you for your heartfelt honesty throughout the entire process of writing. Your patience was off the chart! I absolutely appreciate you helping me, educating me, and encouraging me to dig a little deeper. I hope you know how intelligent and incredible you are. With all my heart, thank you!

Thank you to all of the physicians, nurses, clinic techs, teachers, aids, and therapists who have worked with Jocelyn. Every interaction has led us to where we are today, and without you, that wouldn't be possible.

To the Jocelyn's Journey board and committee, you give me unmeasurable strength. It is because of your hard work that Jocelyn's Journey thrives.

To Rylee and Abigail, thank you for your patience with Daddy and I. We understand things aren't always easy. We love you very much and you make our family complete!

To my husband. Dennis, "thank you" just doesn't say enough for my heartfelt gratitude for always having my back. Even with this. I know it's been rough, but I honestly feel there is nothing we cannot overcome together. You have always been my biggest cheerleader and I love you with all that I am!

And last, but not least, to Jocelyn. Sissy, thank you for being who you are! You are absolutely perfect in every way. I am a better person because of you! You have made such an impact on this world and Daddy and I couldn't be more proud of the brave, strong, determined, happy girl that you are. We love you so much!

# Contents

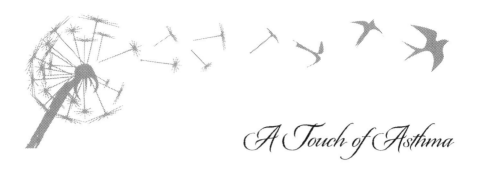

4:01 pm I instructed Crystal to start walking "Let's go!"

"But there's traffic on highway 710, not everyone is here yet." Crystal argued.

"I need myself, Dennis, the officiant and God present- that is it! Let's go!" Crystal shrugged her shoulders and looked at me like "whatever, it's your wedding" then lead the string of my 4 girlfriends down the isle. *I've waited 7 years for this moment, I'm not waiting another minute,* I thought to myself.

Dennis and I started dating when I was 19 and he was 22. We, somewhat, grew up together during that time. A few hiccups that young love experiences, but we made it. We knew we were meant to be together. Before we'd even talk about getting married Dennis wanted to be secure in his firefighter career and own a home. He wanted me to be done with school and well into my career as well. That, in our opinion, was "the right way to do it". We wanted to do things right! So, I graduated with my Bachelors in Science in Nursing in June, 2006. Dennis proposed that Christmas. Check, check, and check. We were confident that our marriage would be amazing, with less struggles because we took the time and effort to do things "right".

It took us 6 months to plan our dream wedding. We wanted everything perfect, "do it right the first time so it's the only time," we'd say. 200 guests, Dennis wanted to be married by the beach, I wanted to be married in the Catholic church. We were both raised catholic, even though we never went to church. I wanted that to be different once we were married though. I also remember being told that God doesn't recognize a marriage unless it is in the Catholic church. Well, I wanted God to recognize our marriage, so we had to follow that rule! I figured after we were married and life calmed down a bit, then maybe we'd start going to church. And if not, we definitely would when we had kids. Check! Check! Check! We were well on our way to doing everything right! Onward to our "happily ever after"!

I grabbed the arm of the strongest, smartest, bravest and gentlest man I will ever know- my grandpa! Before the double doors opened, for our grand entrance to the large catholic sanctuary, Grandpa leaned in and whispered to me, "Have a wonderful life together!" That's when it hit me- this is it! My life with Dennis starts here with these next steps. I was fighting the tears, trying to avoid ruining my make up. I no longer wanted to run down the isle and into the arms of Dennis, I suddenly wanted to marinade in this moment, every second, every emotion. The doors opened. I was ready!

As I walked down the isle, the first person I noticed was Fire Captain Bob sitting on the groom's side. I gazed all the way down, what seemed to be a mile long of pews, searching to find my "almost husband". All I could see at the end was Dennis' mom, Sally- all pretty and proud. That's when I realized the significance: I'm not only marrying Dennis, but I'm marrying into a brotherhood of fireman as well as the entire Jones family! I'll take it! I soaked in every step down the isle, as getty as a child. Before that moment, I just saw the isle walk as "a rite of passage", but in that moment, it suddenly meant so much more. I was living my dream, that very moment. I was almost Dennis' wife, a Jones, marrying into a fire family… I was so ready!

Finally, I saw Dennis! So handsome! Not appearing to be nervous, just bashful that all attention was on him. I was a performing ballerina for 20 years so having eyes on me didn't bother me a bit- unless I had to speak. We walked through the ceremony, like the dance we had rehearsed the night before. Then, it was time to speak- uh oh, I forgot my lines. Father Paul asked us to memorize our vows! I spaced! I was so focused on planning the event that the most important part of it, I had paid the least attention to. What was I thinking?! Too late now, I froze. Dennis had to whisper my lines to me and I let him feed me every word. Oh how embarrassing. But we got through it. I was so relieved that Dennis was bailing me out, literally from the very start of our marriage. I decided it was a good sign of a strong marriage, me letting him calmly lead and getting us through.

Then came the Rite of Catholic Marriage. I realized I had to speak again and I couldn't remember what I was supposed to say: "I do" or "I will". Just as nervous sweat beads were starting to form under my giant white dress, Dennis took the lead again, "I will" he said to the first question and I muttered a quick "I will" right behind him. Several questions came and went and we proclaimed "I will" in uniform to all of them. But one question came at me like an arrow to the heart:

"Will you accept children lovingly from God and bring them up according to the law of Christ and his Church?" Father Paul asked. "I will" I immediately replied and then my thoughts drifted to Aunt Tammy.

When I was 10, she and my Uncle Bary were going through the process of adopting children because they weren't physically able to have their own. One of the questions she had to answer was, whether she would accept a child with medical problems. Even at the young age of 10 I felt how difficult this must be for a prospecting parent to answer. Not for the fact of it being physically or financially draining on a parent, but what parent wants to see their child suffer with ANYTHING?! I remember she jokingly answered, "a touch of asthma I could handle".

I returned to the alter from my daydream. This question from the Catholic Rite of Marriage felt like Aunt Tammy's adoption application. In my giant white dress, 6 inch hills and 200 people staring at me: "Will I accept children lovingly from God…"? Well Aunt Tammy ended up adopting two happy healthy boys so it worked for her. So I silently added onto my "I will" what Aunt Tammy said. *I'm cool with a touch of asthma, Lord. Yes, a touch of asthma we could handle. Not severe though, okay? Just a touch. We want our kids to be able to play sports and stuff.* I then sighed with relief at my silent prayer, as if I just clicked "submit" on my application for children with God and continued with the dance of our ceremony. "I now pronounce you husband and wife". Finally! WE DID IT!

## The Empty Carseat

It was August in California. Hot. Dennis was digging trenches for our new sprinkler system. Only two months as "newly weds", we were excited about our combined income and ready to get the house the way we wanted with landscaping, decorating, and furniture. The luxury of the nurse/fireman schedule allowed us to have a stretch of days off together that we could plan quick get-aways to the river or Las Vegas. This was the life! This was great! Our plan was going just as we had expected.

I walked out a glass of ice cold water to my hard working new husband. I could tell he enjoyed working on his yard, but I couldn't understand how he tolerated such heat while doing so. I watched him quench his thirst. For the first time in my life I was at a loss for words. Terrified to talk. My heart was racing, eventually I was able to blurt out: "I'm pregnant." There was no hesitation from Dennis as he instantly dropped the shovel and sped walked to me and gave me a hug. I didn't know what to expect, but I didn't expect that. I was still terrified even though he was hugging me. I don't remember if he was smiling or not because I still had the "deer in the headlights" that had been plastered on my face since I left the bathroom, 10 minutes prior. When he stopped hugging me his confusion seemed to set in too: "Are you sure?" he finally mumbled out. It's so funny how guys are in denial until they're actually holding their baby, but moms become moms the moment the stick turns pink!

"Well, I didn't draw a line on the stick, trying to trap you" I answered with my typical jerk sarcasm. This was exciting, I guess. Most of our friends were pregnant. We were both over 25. I guess that's the "right" time to start. But we didn't plan this! This was supposed to be in a year or two. After we were married for a bit. The thought definitely took some getting used to, for both of us.

Telling other people was almost as hard as telling Dennis. We waited until the first trimester was over. Working in the emergency room for over 4 years, I had seen and helped women every single day deal with spontaneous abortions, aka miscarriages. Extremely common in the first trimester. The controversy was that some would argue that miscarriages are on the rise, but the opposing argument was that they are the same as they always have been, women are just finding out sooner that they are pregnant. Time and time again, at least a few a day in the ER, I saw young women who just found out they were pregnant, coming to the hospital for bleeding and most would turn out to be, spontaneous abortions. The moms look to us for help, but there is nothing we could do for their loss. It was imbedded into me that if there are any complications during pregnancy, "it is not a viable fetus until 20 weeks gestation" so efforts to save a pregnancy or the fetus before then, were simply not done. With the surprise of the test, then all this negative knowledge and experience with pregnant women, it was hard to swallow it all. I was adamant that I wouldn't tell anyone until my first trimester was over. I didn't want to be the fool and be excited about a baby to be, just to loose the pregnancy as I've witnessed so many times in my career. The loss would be devastating, but to have to everyone who knew I was pregnant that it was a loss, that would make it even worse. To have people watch me grieve and they themselves grieve too. I just didn't want any part of that. So I remained in literally nauseating silence for months.

At 12 weeks I finally allowed myself to get excited. I was almost done with my first trimester, so I felt safe- in the clear of a miscarriage! That was when I went for my first ultrasound appointment. I had to go alone because Dennis was at work. As soon as the monitor screen turned on, that was it! I fell in love instantly! This weird looking alien on the monitor was waving its little arms around as if practicing kung fu! I couldn't believe how active this little being was and I couldn't feel anything! It was so cool! I couldn't wait to show Dennis the pictures. I couldn't wait for him to get home so I paid him a visit at the fire station to show him pictures, share with him what I saw. I was disappointed that he wasn't as excited as I was yet. He still had a bit of the "deer in headlight" look.

A week later we went on a pre-pregnancy planned trip to Mexico with the Jones'. I was not too thrilled about going to Mexico, pregnant, where they have "dirty" water. I was cautious about everything there. I lived on orange soda- also probably not the best thing, but I figured 5 days of it was better than harming my baby with something in the water. Microbiology in nursing school ruined me! Or saved me! I wouldn't eat fruit from vendors on the streets, I barely got in the swimming pool at our hotel, I got motion sickness on tours... I was probably very annoying to our travel buddies, but I honestly didn't care. If something were to happen to the baby or the pregnancy because I went to Mexico, I would've never forgiven myself. I was extremely cautious of everything, despite the appropriate eye rolling of others. However, one of the best things that ever happen to me, happened on this trip: I finally felt my baby move! It felt like something scratching or tickling my lower abdomen, from the inside. All I could imagine was the little alien doing kung fu and using my uterus as a wall to do back flips- martial arts style. I was so proud and protective of my little alien and if that bothered anyone- oh well.

When I was 8 months pregnant I experienced my first sleepless night as a mother. Usually, I had no trouble sleeping at all while pregnant. According to Dennis, I would be so out that my snore could shake the house. I would say it's a lie but time and time again, he'd wake me up terrified and explain "you were snoring!" Poor guy- his new bride turned into a large snoring, mumu wearing, beast in a matter of months. So for me not being able to sleep was very strange!

I reflected on the events of that day- my baby shower. It was beautifully decorated, the food was amazing and over 80 women came! We had all of my friends and both sides of the family pile into, the soon-to-be Grandma, Sally's living room. We made the shower a big deal and used the attention to announce what we were going to name our little girl! I made personalized buttons for the grandparents and Dennis and I. Mine read "Mommy to be, for Jocelyn Emily" and everyone's said the same with their title. If there was Pinterest back then, I would've got 200 pins. I was so proud of my creativity, not just in the name we chose, but in how we announced it. The meaning of Jocelyn is what I loved the most "joyful and happy".

There were many gifts, cards filled with love. I remember my big ol' belly kept getting in the way as I had to lean over and get the next goodie bag. No more room for kung fu now, little one! I was exhausted during the day, so I couldn't figure out, why in the world could I not sleep that night?

I recalled every person smiling, rubbing my belly, telling me they couldn't wait to hold my little girl. The cards I read all exclaimed how much they loved our daughter and what a blessing she is... Then, I finally realized in the shadows of 2am why I couldn't sleep- I was jealous! This was mine and Dennis' baby, BUT I had to share her! So many other people already loved her too! Tears and tears streamed down my face- I didn't want to share her! She was ours! It took me months to share, with even the grandparents, what her name was going to be. And all these people wanted to hold her, love on her, take her out for ice cream and the movies when she was old enough?! I hadn't thought this through! We stayed living in our small town because we wanted to raise our kids where our families were. But now, I felt sad that I had to share her!

I started thinking about how I grew up. My parents divorced when I was 8 and my dad wasn't in the picture much after that. My grandparents helped watch my brother and I while my mom worked nights at the hospital, as a registered nurse. The Dechant family was close with my mom when she was in high school and they also helped out with watching my brother, Jason, and I. They became our extended family, we still refer to them as aunts, uncles, cousins and grandparents. We loved spending time with them growing up and it was always a treat to visit them. Having extended family didn't make me love my mom any less, it just well rounded me. We got to go to the lake with Debbie, Big Bear with Lori, Grandpa John had Jason help hand Christmas lights every year while I was inside helping Grandma Shirley wrap presents. We always had a blast no matter which Dechant we were visiting with. But, I always wanted to come home and home was with my mom. So why would my baby be any different if she had extra people to love on her and make her well rounded by offering different life experiences?

A few hours in the dark, rocking my big belly in the oversized recliner chair with puffy eyes and tears, I finally made peace with myself that it was okay that other people loved Jocelyn too. I could share her- a little! With a few people- but lets not get crazy now! She was still mine and Dennis'! No one else's! But I guess they could love her too.

Despite preterm labor at 24 weeks, which resulted in me going on maternity leave, I was now 41 weeks with no progression suggestive of labor. Oh I was so sad! I cried in my OB's office and went home and soothed myself with a bean and cheese burrito. Despite the discomfort of feeling enormous, I wanted Jocelyn home- she was late. I was upset with her as if she were being rude! We were all ready, her room was done, plenty of diapers, the house was spotless… it was time!! Later that night, my doctor called and agreed to induce me the following week. I was so excited! I hoped she would come naturally before then, but if not, we had a plan. I'm a planner- having a plan comforted me more than the bean and cheese burrito I just devoured.

The week took forever to pass, but it finally did. We went to the hospital, excited and ready to bring home our baby! It felt strange staring at an empty carseat, knowing she would be in it soon. I had the outfit we would bring her home in all picked out. I brought 2 outfits, just in case she was bigger than expected. Tiny diapers were in our brand new diaper bag, which I FINALLY got to carry. This was exciting, finally, I get to meet her, to hold her!

After paperwork, an IV and an epidural, things were going according to plan. I was having major contractions and couldn't feel a thing. "Beep beep beep" her heart beat went. I remembered some of the equipment in the room from nursing school, but not much. I was into emergency care- OB nursing grossed me out so I just jumped through the hoops for school and had academic bulimia for most of that curriculum.

While we waited for the induction medication to move things along, Dennis and I were playing our usual card game, Skip-Bo. It was only 7pm but I kept falling asleep like I was a narcoleptic. It made sense, even though I couldn't feel pain and contractions, my body was still going through the trauma of labor and needed rest. After Dennis won, yet another game,

I intermittently slept. I thought I felt a contraction at one point, looked over at the monitor, and sure enough, I was in the middle of one. During it, I noticed Jocelyn's heart rate going down. I strived to remember from school, what that meant- was that trouble or normal? Then my narcolepsy took over and I was asleep again. Confusion consumed me, but I couldn't stay awake long enough to reason through my concerns.

Minutes later, the nurse came in and looked at the paper recorded monitor strip I was just studying, then she hurriedly walked out of my room. After yet another 20 second narcoleptic nap, I awoke to see my nurse next to me with 3 other nurses, the doctor, and the anesthesiologist. They were looking at the monitor talking softly to each other. I may not have known how to read the monitor at the moment, but working in the ER for 5 years, I could definitely recognize a medical "UH-OH" look.

And every person in the room had one. "What's going on?" I finally demanded.

The doctor finally looked over at me and got into "catch" position. "Mrs. Jones, the baby's heart rate is dropping and she might be in trouble. We need to get her out right now, I need you to push!" I heard a hint of panic, as well as a sense of urgency in his voice. I followed his instruction and did what I was told. The nurses helped coach me on what to do and held my numb legs. My legs looked as though they were someone else's as I watched them being grabbed and pulled, but I couldn't feel anything. The confusion of how to push in combination with numbness and my worry for my baby made the entire ordeal horrible. This was not the plan! This was not foreseen or expected! I tried so hard to push and be a good patient for over two minutes until they had me stop to listen for Jocelyn's heart rate.

"Did I do it? Did I help?" I asked one of the nurses.

"You're doing fine, every things ok" she calmly and quietly tried to reassure me while holding my hand. Then as she turned, I could read her panicked face as she darted to the other side of the room for something.

The room was silent while we all listened for Jocelyn's heart beat. Suddenly, the doctor unlocked my bed and the team rushed my bed out of the room. The doctor explained, "We have to get the baby out right now. We are going to the OR for a C-section." Then he quickly spat out what I recognized as a verbal consent and I agreed to whatever he said.

A C-section was definitely not what we had planed on, however, Jocelyn was in danger, so I was suddenly okay with the change of plans.

Dennis calmly followed.

"Get the camera" I yelled at him.

Plan for the worst, expect the best- that's what we do in emergency medicine. Best case, we will be holding our baby soon and taking pictures. As they whipped me down the hallways, I had a heart to heart with God about the worst case:

*Just let me hold her! I want to see her alive, I want her to see me, God, PLEASE!* I prayed silently with my eyes closed. *I know it is not possible to trade her spots, but if it were, take me! Dennis is such a good man. He could take great care of her. If you do take me, can I just stay long enough to hold her, to meet her?*

"You guys, you do realize this is a CRASH C-section?!! What are you doing?!" the doctor demanded to his crew as they were trying to untangle my IV tubes from my epidural and other monitor wires. I lay there quietly, continuing my plead with God. Then I remembered Jocelyn's car seat. The empty car seat. The one I was so excited to put her in, was now in danger of staying empty. Tears streamed down my cheeks in the chaotic room. I didn't just want to hold her, I wanted to see Dennis hold her. I've gotten to be with her for over 40 weeks, feeling kicks and hiccups and her "kung fu". 24/7 I was with her, my heart broke that Dennis wouldn't get to be alone with her. To and fall in love as much as I had.

Thinking of Dennis, I realized he still wasn't in the room. I was so worried that he was calmly staying out of the way in some waiting room and that the panic team had forgotten about him. I wanted him in the room! I had toughed out being alone for the IV and epidural, which I was nervous and scared about- especially the epidural! But I was done being brave- I wanted my husband with me! I was strapped to a table numb from the waist down and completely helpless and loosing hope. I started to panic as I saw a sterile tray of tools get brought out. Large blue, sterile drapes quickly flung over me and taped down left me with only a view of the ceiling. I felt some pulling on my lower abdomen.

"I feel that! I feel that!" I told the anesthesiologist who was working at the head of my bed.

Ignoring me, the anesthesiologist yelled to the doctor who was about to cut me open "Doc, she says she can feel it. I can tube her, you want me to tube her?" Which means he wanted to completely knock me out and put a tube down my throat in order to breathe for me.

"You're not tubing me!" I scolded the anesthesiologist. "I know what that means! I want to hear my baby's first cry".

The doctor seemed annoyed as if we were siblings fighting over who was right. "Stop! Elizabeth, do you feel this?"

"Umm, a little" I nervously answered.

"This? Is it pressure or sharp?"

"Just pressure a little."

"That's fine, you are fine, I'm cutting," he busily growled at me.

Finally, Dennis appeared wearing a yellow jump suite and made his way to my head. Nervous and relieved, tears rolled down my cheeks uncontrollably. I couldn't wipe them away with my hands tied to the bed. He wiped a few tears for me and scratched my nose for me. He was so calm. It annoyed me. But I was happy he was finally with me. I wasn't alone anymore. He would make sure everything went smoothly.

"Do you have the camera?" I asked, trying to be positive while killing the silence between us.

"Yes, Beth. Relax, it's okay" he calmly said. Moments later he leaned in and whispered to me, "I like totally see all your guts all over the place."

"Thanks babe" I rolled my eyes and chuckled inside. Such a bonehead, fireman thing to say. That's when I knew he was nervous too- trying to make light of everything.

Then, a cry!

"SHE'S OUT, SHE'S OUT!" the doctor yelled with relief.

I heard the sweetest sound- her cry! Suddenly, my tears were coming with the most interesting noises from deep within me, somewhat resembling a hyena. I felt overwhelming calmness pour over me as I continued to hear my baby cry! She was breathing on her own! Her heart was beating on it's own! Jocelyn Emily had entered the world loudly, and I couldn't have been more elated!

"7 pounds, 1 ounce. 19 inches," I heard the nurse yell from the other side of the room.

I loved hearing her. I was so proud of her weight and height. The sad, worried cries were suddenly changed to happy, proud cries.

Dennis got the "okay" from a nurse to come to her and take pictures while they cleaned up Jocelyn. I remained strapped to the bed and sat quietly, listening intently to every little noise she made. Dennis came back to my head and I asked 20 questions "How's her color? Is she okay? What do you think?..." Just then, a nurse came around the drape and showed me my precious, swaddled baby! She was perfect. Big cheeks like Daddy! It was incredible. She was alive! I was alive! I waved my restrained hand at her "HI" as the tears poured down. Jocelyn answered with a weak moan that resembled a cat. I chuckled at the adorable noises. The nurse told me she would take her to the recovery room and wait for me there.

"Follow her Dennis, and don't let her out of your sight!" I demanded-my first bout of separation anxiety, I realized, but didn't care.

"Yes dear" he calmly obliged.

What felt like days later, I was wheeled to recovery and I got what I begged God for. I got to hold my baby! She was so tiny and perfect, with long fingers. She was just good! Beautiful! I was so happy, I couldn't do anything but stare. *Thank you God! Thank you, thank you, thank you!* I repeatedly silently prayed for hours, maybe days. I got to hold her, and I'm still holding her! She is fine, I am fine, Dennis is a little green, but he'll be fine! Everything was perfect.

# Chuck One Up for Me!

The few two days with our new baby were like a peaceful dream. Jocelyn was such a beautiful "glow worm" I called her when the nurses swaddled her all up with her tiny beanie on. She nursed well, she barely cried. She would eat, sleep, and …. yeah, you guessed it! All the plumbing was in full effect. Her first demonstration was at almost 12 hours of life. Since I conveniently couldn't completely feel my legs yet from the epidural, it was all on Dennis. I chuckled in bed at his facial expressions while he gagged! He was on his 5th diaper of the same episode of elimination, he finally exclaimed: "Are you SERIOUS?! It keeps coming! I don't understand how something so small had so much in her! What in the world is going on!"

Now I'm laughing in bed, but trying not to because my incision hurt when I laughed.

"It's not funny! Do you want to get over here and do this?!" he yelled at me, which of course made me laugh harder. Then I could hear the most adorable, tinniest little noise which resembled the grunt of a puppy.

"Are you kidding me?!" Dennis screamed to the world, through the window, arms stretched up while Jocelyn laid in her hospital baby bed, doing her "thing". If Dennis could handle this, he was going to be great at fatherhood! Despite his disgust, I was was so proud of him for following through and cleaning up his little 7 pound (maybe 6 pound by now) bundle of joy.

The next day, we were all bundled up, ready to go. Jocelyn was fed and we were waiting on discharge paperwork. I was standing with Jocelyn, swaddled in my arms, and I looked over at her. She seemed to be struggling.

"Dennis!" I panicked and called him over to look at Jocelyn.

"Is she breathing?" he asked.

"I don't know, go get her nurse!" I demanded as I started lay her on my bed to unwrap her from her swaddle.

"I can't find her nurse," Dennis peaked his head back in the room.

"Get any nurse!" I screamed. "Call a code! Do something!" and he ran out. Once I had her out of her swaddle, I picked her up, and like a fountain she projectile spit up all over. Then we both started crying as Dennis came in with a nurse. The nurse, very concerned, began asking a million questions while doing an assessment on Jocelyn. Listening to her lungs, checking circulation. I was mute, I couldn't find the words to explain what happened. I was struggling in my own head to rationalize what just happened. When I finally was able to speak, I told Dennis and the nurse, "She was choking". The nurse said she looked good and would call the doctor and let him know what happened. Then our assigned nurse walked in.

"What happened?" she asked.

"She was choking and then had a projectile spit up," I explained.

"Okay," she answered calmly. "When was the last time she ate?"

"She finished 10 minutes ago."

"Well how long did she nurse for?"

"About 20 minutes each side" I explained.

"That is too long!" she firmly educated. "She is a newborn and doesn't need to eat for that long. Do not let her treat you like a pacifier or she will get too full and things like what just happened will happen! Did you burp her?"

"No," I admitted. I wanted so bad to lie! All the books I read said that breastfed babies will eat until they have had enough and don't really need to burp. I studied! I researched! I thought I was doing it right.

"She needs to be burped! Between sides and half way through if she is eating for a long time. Every 10 minutes is a good rule!" she continued to lecture.

"Okay, got it" I just wanted her to shut up and go away. I wanted to go home. When I first saw the projectile spit up, the ER nurse in me was thinking pyloric stenosis- which is diagnosed in newborns and is symptom based. Pyloric stenosis is narrowing of the valve between the stomach and the small intestine, causing food to sit in the stomach. And having no where else to go, like a fountain, it will come back out the mouth. It is typically found in newborns during the first few weeks of life. I've had multiple patients in the ER who we were ruling out "pyloric stenosis" due to projectile vomiting. But if Jocelyn's episode was my mistake in not burping her, and it wasn't pyloric stenosis, then I could live with that.

Finally, about an hour later, we were well on our way home, exhausted from the emotional roller coaster of the last 3 days, but excited to get into the routine of being a family. I sat in the back seat with our precious cargo next to me in her carseat. I reflected on my labor with Jocelyn, a few nights prior, and was suddenly overfilled with gratitude and happiness. Our infant carseat was not empty! We had the most beautiful baby in the world filling the carseat, along with our hearts!

Our first night at home as a family of three was finally here! I gave her her first bath, well, sponge bath, in our master bathroom. The smell of baby lotion, which I would inhale while pregnant and day dream about holding Jocelyn, was actually being used on her. This was the moment I had dreamed of for months now. She smelled so fresh, pure, calm, beautiful. I bundled her in a pair of footie pj's with tiny flowers on them. Dennis came around the corner at the same time and we met in the doorway between our bathroom and bedroom, he kissed her on her head and breathed her in. My six foot one, 200 pound macho fireman husband whispered to his sweet daughter, "What did we ever do without you?" It is a moment I will remember forever! I thought I loved Dennis the most I ever could the day we got married, but this just took it to the next level. This was amazing, our little family! The love in the room was so intense, I felt like I was floating!

We were all asleep for maybe 30 minutes when a high pitched beeping alarm screamed at us. It was coming from my side of the bed and startled me. I jumped and felt a horrible tear at my incision. I physically could not sit up. "DENNIS- GET HER!" I realized it was Jocelyn's SIDS monitor alarming in the cradle next to my side of the bed.

Working in the emergency room for 5 years comes with the unfortunate life experiences of seeing mortality. Mortality of all ages.

Even babies.

Dennis being a fireman for over 15 years, had also had his share of infant CPR's. It is a brutal picture in your head that you can never shake. I was trained that in emergency medicine, we are to medically give them every opportunity to have spontaneous return of circulation, but ultimately, it is up to God. Unfortunately, the success rate in infant CPR's isn't high at all. Infant CPRs usually end up with the cause of death being Sudden Infant Death Syndrome (SIDS). The peacefully passed infants look like toy dolls. Beautiful, quiet, peaceful, still… but cold. It's the heartbreak of the family that is unbearable. The begging scream from a mother, "BREATH!" or "She was just eating 2 hours ago"… and all you can do is comfort and watch the parents hold their baby's body as they go through the beginning phases of grief.

I've been on the medical side and the personal side of SIDS. I have a cousin who lost a baby to SIDS, and to watch her go through the pain of the loss, even years later, is heart wrenching. I never knew that caskets were made so small until then. It is something most people would rather not speak of, for obvious reasons.

With what Dennis and I had seen and learned, we were avoiding SIDS statistics at all cost. So it was a no brainer that the baby monitor we chose for Jocelyn was a SIDS monitor as well. It wasn't an official medical one- just one that paranoid parents, like ourselves, could get at the local baby store to give ourselves peace of mind. It was a motion detector the size of a mouse pad that went under the mattress and it would alarm if it didn't sense movement (or breathing) for 20 seconds.

As the alarm screamed, I was rolling around on the bed like a turtle on it's back, screaming to Dennis to hurry. After what seemed like a 5 minute sprint around the bed, Dennis finally reached Jocelyn, swooped her up and she spit up all over her precious flower pj's.

"She's breathing!" I sighed with relief.

Dennis helped me sit up and we both unraveled her swaddle, undressed her and each did our own assessment. She started to cry, probably from all the commotion and that she was cold, but she looked fine. We changed her outfit, swaddled her back up and tried to go back to bed. Before Dennis rolled over he instructed me, "Just make sure you burp her good when she gets up for her next feed."

"Are you serious?! I do burp her. Don't you think after the hospital episode I would make sure I burp her?!" I barked.

"I'm not saying you didn't burp her, Beth. I'm just saying maybe it was a stuck burp" then he rolled over and fell asleep. I propped myself high up with pillows in case I was needed again during the night.

Two hours later, Jocelyn woke to feed, and a diaper change. She was such a good baby. No fuss, right to business then back to sleep. I burped her and we were good. As I laid her down, she woke up. I picked her up, she fell asleep- "GREAT" I thought, "I'm already spoiling her at 3 days old!" I laid her back down to see if she'd sooth herself to sleep again. I read in one of my many pregnancy and parenting books that it could happen. And she did! I was so proud of myself. I turned the lights off and was about to fall asleep when I heard her fussing. Lights back on and she was drenched with spit up!

With great defeat, I woke up Dennis. "Babe, I can't do this! I need to sleep. She was fed! She needs to be changed again and her bed too this time. Maybe I over fed her. I need you to get up so I can at least have 30 minutes of sleep, please!" I begged.

"Did you burp her?" he simply asked. I took it as a complete insult and ignored his question. He got at least a few hours in and he wasn't about to lecture me.

*I just had surgery! I need rest to heal!* I thought to myself. I heard him talk sweetly to his daughter as he changed her clothes, and bedding and I was quickly sound asleep.

This dance was our every night for a week. We went to the breastfeeding clinic to see if I was doing something wrong. They did an assessment of what I was eating and everything checked out okay. Jocelyn was gaining weight, had wet diapers, looked good, and we were doing just fine. They looked at us like adorable new parents who didn't have a clue.

"She's just a spit up baby" they tried to reassure us. It just didn't seem right though. My nephew was a bad spit up baby, but nothing like this. The difference- he was on formula! It had to be me! But I didn't want to give up. "Breast is the best" is in every parenting class, book, pediatrician's office… you name it. I wanted the best for my daughter, but was I not the best?

*Am I being prideful?* I worried.

"You and I were 'formula babies' and we are just fine, Jocelyn could be a 'formula baby' too- I support whatever you want to do," Dennis would constantly tell me, trying to stay out of the internal struggle I would have during every feed.

At about 2 weeks old, with medical advice offering no solutions, I realized I had to change something. I was so tired of the SIDS monitor, sheet changing dance 5 times a night. I moved out of the bedroom with Jocelyn and set up camp on our oversized recliner chair. There, I would change her diaper, feed her, burp, then she would snuggle and sleep- sitting upright- on my chest. It was the best thing in the world! I was finally getting sleep, and so was she. Her food was staying down! I had never been more in love with gravity. I outsmarted the midnight spit up dance! My first victory as a mom!

# MCI (Multi-Casualty Incident)

I may have won the night-time spit up battle, however, Jocelyn's spit ups were just as bad during the day and I couldn't hold her all day and night. At her 4 week check up the doctor didn't like the small amount of weight Jocelyn was gaining. The first label from a doctor was not a pretty one: "FAILURE TO THRIVE"!

*Failure? FAILURE?! Are you kidding me?* I thought. *But I out smarted it! We were sleeping, she is pooping and peeing. We are good.* I didn't think FAILURE should be used anywhere in our family for what we overcame those first four weeks. The midnight bickering between Dennis and I about "did you burp her" or not. Or "It's your turn to change the sheets," 2 am dilemma. Or "Seriously, Dennis? You only packed 5 outfits in the diaper bag to change her after she spits? You knew we were going to be gone for 2 hours. You should know by now that isn't enough changes"… FAILURE?

I knew exactly what "failure to thrive" meant medically. But I was on the other side of it. WE were being labeled as FAILURES! A horrible thing to tell a sleep deprived mother who was struggling to keep enough food in her baby- knowing she has been the only source of nutrition. So if the nutrition aspect of my daughter's life was FAILING- there was only one person to blame- ME!

At 4 weeks we introduced formula to Jocelyn. We were told it might be "heavier" and could stay down more easily. "My milk is too thin and watery and my pride of keeping her on breast milk has caused her heart burn for the first 4 weeks of life" was all I heard. I cried and cried when Dennis gave Jocelyn her first bottle. DEFEATED. I FAILED my child. Once the bottle was done, she passed out like a crazy uncle after

Thanksgiving dinner! I felt further defeated. She looked so comfortable. We tested the waters and laid her down in her pack-n-play. She was good. She was sleeping great! Dennis and I agreed she would have formula at night, and "mommy milk" in the daytime.

Two hours into her first formula slumber she started coughing. We picked her up and spit up shot right out of her tiny mouth. I have to admit, I was somewhat gloating inside that, just maybe, it wasn't me! The gloating was quickly overcome with worry. *Now what?* Formula was the only solution Dennis and I had. We still stuck to our decision to give night time formula a chance.

As weeks passed, Jocelyn was sleeping better at night with less spit ups. Finally, at 3 months, I decided she had had enough of the early antibodies from "mommy's milk" and could be transitioned to 100% formula. I thought for sure this would end the 5 outfits in the diaper bag for a trip to the store and the bickering between Dennis and I of who burps her more or better. We were moving on from this spit up mess! Formula it is! But our hopes were crushed. It wasn't the end. In fact, it stayed the same. Then I began torturing myself for stopping breastfeeding too soon.

It was July now and I was grateful for the warm California weather. We let our beautiful girl lounge around the house naked while dish towels were readily on hand, waiting for the clean up of her reflux. However we had a huge accomplishment to one of our struggles- she was finally sleeping through the night!

At four months old, Jocelyn was still spitting up. We were then referred to a gastrointestinal specialist. The label FAILURE to thrive continued to follow us. Jocelyn could now hold her own bottle, she smiled and "coo'ed" and Dennis and I were more in love than ever! We just hurt for our baby, imagining the heartburn she must have felt every single day, even though she probably didn't know any better. For being such a happy baby, we decided she probably thought it was normal. But we wanted more for our daughter than to think that constant heartburn and discomfort was normal.

Jocelyn also wasn't rolling around on the floor as much as our friends babies did at her age. Both my maid of honors, Crystal and Kristin, were pregnant during our wedding. Their babies, Mckenzie and Jacob, were sitting up at four months old. Sure they would wobble like Weebles, but Jocelyn was no where near ready for an attempt at Weeble position. Dennis and I reasoned that it was because we didn't give her enough tummy time. We were FAILING at that because once Jocelyn was fed, we treated her like porcelain. With a full tummy, we sat her in a reclined position and dared not startle her because we knew the chances of our hard work could result in it coming right back out in a split second.

So in the GI specialist's office we sat and agreed to try some medication for the reflux. I absolutely hated the idea of medication for a 4 month old, but I also hated the idea of anymore FAILURES. We obliged and started her on an acid reducer, as well as another one I will call "Medication XXX" which was supposed to increase gastric emptying rate. We started her on low doses and hoped for the best.

By day two of medication, Jocelyn was screaming like never before. "Medication XXX" had a side effect of fatigue so I figured she was just tired. She went down early for her morning nap, then her afternoon nap, then an even earlier bedtime. *She's just adjusting to the meds*, I reassured myself. Day three came and the screaming came with vengeance. The screaming and crying led to her spitting up even more than usual. Night three, I skipped the bedtime dose of "Medication XXX" and held my exhausted 4 month old. This time it was me crying my eyes out apologizing to her for what I put her through. I thought I was helping her, but it was torturous. We decided to keep her on the acid reducer which didn't help the spitting up, but if we were decreasing the acid that was coming up with her food all the time, at least we were making life a little bit more comfortable for our daughter.

In October, I took Jocelyn to get her six month pictures and invited Jacob (exactly 1 year) and Mckenzie (10 months) to come with us and we could all take Halloween pictures together. Jacob was a tiger, Mckenzie a spider, and Jocelyn a monkey. They were all so cute and us mommy's (best friends since high school) were so proud of our adorable children. This is what the three of us talked about, dreamed about- our kids growing up together. Along with the excitement of a fulfilled dream, another emotion began to fill my heart, one that I knew my two girlfriends did not share with me: envy. I watched Jacob and Mckenzie crawling around the photo room, getting into everything. Meanwhile, I was struggling to have my six month old sit on her own long enough for a picture. "We're a little behind" I explained to the photographer with a chuckle as I sat Jocelyn up, once again stopping her from tipping over. With all the commotion in the room I was secretly praying that she wouldn't spit up all over her expensive costume- or worse, in front of everyone. Finally, we got a few good shots of the three kids and we all parted ways. I felt a little guilty when I sighed with relief after leaving my friends and their "on the go" babies. I just wanted to take Jocelyn home and snuggle into a nap with her- alone!

The following week was her 6 month "well baby check" at the doctors. Dennis and I were both there to console Jocelyn after the vaccinations she was due for. We were waiting for the doctor and we practiced sitting "Baby Jo" in front of the mirror. She loved it! She giggled and played with the noisy exam table tissue paper. She wobbled a bit like a Weeble, but it didn't interrupt the three of us having fun and playing and giggling. Baby Jo had the most adorable, contagious laugh that Dennis and I were so proud of and could never get enough of.

The doctor walked in and was scoping us out. This was a new doctor to us because Jocelyn's first pediatrician moved away. This doctor was in her mid to late 30's. A short, Asian woman who looked like she borrowed her dad's lab coat to "play" doctor. She pulled up her computer and began her assessment questions.

"Do you work?" she asked.

"Yes, we both do- I'm an RN and Dennis is a fireman" I explained.

"Who watches Jocelyn while you are at work?"

"We trade off so it's only us watching her. If we both work the same day, Dennis' mom watches her."

"Does anyone smoke around the baby?" she snipped back.

"No"

She clicked, clicked, clicked on her keyboard while Dennis and I continued the mirror tissue paper game with our adorable little girl. *How can this doctor not laugh? Jocelyn's laugh was incredibly contagious,* I thought to myself. The doctor kept her stern face and was all business. *This doctor is too young to be so prudish*, I thought.

Finally, the doctor came over to Jocelyn and had an awkward baby talk.

"Hi Jocelyn" she said attempting to engage. Jocelyn just looked blankly at her.   Dennis and I gazed at each other with a chuckle in our eyes, proud of our daughter not being fond of "Doctor Prude". The doctor laid her down, listened to her heart, lungs, looked in her ears… When she started to assess and palpate her adorable tummy, I cringed, afraid that she would force a spit up out. *Please God, Please God, NO!* and sure enough "blahh" a spit up. Dennis quickly wiped her up with a cloth we always kept within a 1 foot radius of Jocelyn.

"We are already seeing the GI specialist about that. She is on an acid reducer medication," I explained quickly.

"Oh, yeah, I noticed she is a little under weight on the growth chart," she mentioned.

"Yes, but she is gaining from the last visit so we are progressing."

"Is she sitting up and rolling yet," she asked, ignoring my last comment.

"She can almost sit up, and yes she has rolled before."

"Both back to tummy and tummy to back," she snapped, demanding clarification.

"Just tummy to back" I admitted. I could feel my face start to turn red. I've always been horrible at hiding what I am thinking. You can literally read my thoughts on my face.

"Oh!" she exclaimed as if she suddenly saw a spider in the room. "Was she born full term?"

"Yes."

"Any problems during pregnancy? Did you drink? Any drugs?" she accused, looking for a reason for all the red flags she was observing.

"No!" I defended.

Now I felt Dennis getting uncomfortable. Dennis is a man of few words, but when he does speak up, he means business and the situation can turn really uncomfortable. Especially when he is witnessing his wife getting backed into a corner.

"She seems really floppy. Low tone" Doctor Prude thought to herself, out loud, then went back to her computer to look at her chart. "Hmmm, FAILURE to thrive. Well yes," she agreed with the computer.

I could feel my heart racing in my chest. My thoughts pounded in my head turning my complexion almost purple: *Anyone else uses the word*

*FAILURE today, I'm going to loose it! How about the doctor failing to notice how perfect she is. How her giggle is the best in the world. Failure to notice her button nose, the bow in her hair, her love for her own reflection, as babies so curiously do.* I took a few deep breaths and stepped in between Dennis and the doctor, hoping positioning in the room would refrain him from speaking up. If he started, he wouldn't quit and if that happened, I was certain we would be escorted out of the building.

The doctor broke the silence: "Does she have CP?"

The room fell silent and a thick cloud of darkness filled every cubic inch in the room. It paralyzed me.

The doctor thought she needed to speak slower, as if we didn't hear her, "Are-you-sure-she-doesn't-have-cerebral-palsy"?

"NO! She does NOT" I replied just as slow as the question came. *Am I sure? Oh I could've smacked her! Did she not hear me tell her when she first walked in that I'm an RN? I'm pretty sure if someone even breathed to me a diagnosis of CP, I'd remember! What kind of idiot was touching my child! The only thing we've been told was that we were FAILING- but I could fix that! Failure was not an option and I am determined to break that label off of us!*

"Well, she might have CP- I'm going to order Occupational Therapy. Someone will contact you in a week to schedule her sessions. Here's a copy of the growth chart that she isn't really on, because of the FAILURE to thrive. Continue to follow up with the GI doctor for the reflux. Do you have any questions for me?" she quickly stated with her hand on the doorknob- oblivious to the train that just hit and crushed Dennis and I.

"NO! You can leave now!" Dennis spat at her. Clueless of his hatred for her, she exited the room.

The car ride home was silent. Jocelyn fell asleep. I quietly wiped my tears in the passenger seat while Dennis skimmed the radio, trying to find a good song to drown out all the noise we had just heard.

*Tough Love*

The struggle at home became very routine. Feed, spit up, bath/mop, nap, repeat. Occasionally we dared to try and break routine and go do something normal, like going out to dinner with our friends and their kids. The other kids sat in their carseats or highchairs and were handed their bottles or sippy cups. Jocelyn would need to be held and fed, burped every ten minutes and was so slow to drink a bottle. It astonished me how quickly my friends kids would pound their milk.

*Surely, that's not normal*, I thought to myself. *Why don't they burp them?* Then their child would sit up and a loud belch would escape while they smiled proudly.

Seeing a baby burp without something coming out was not my normal at all. When Jocelyn would finally suck down her 6 oz bottle, which took 45 minutes, half of it would come shooting out with a burp, messing up whatever cute outfit she had on. I would use all five outfits packed in the diaper bag whenever we dared to go into public. It was exhausting, it smelled, and sure, I got embarrassed and frustrated. I started to become jealous of our friends and the more we were around them, I realized just how hard we had it.

Dennis and I have always been social people and we had always loved having friends around, but the constant reminder of how different Jocelyn was from other children was too much for me to handle. Dennis still wanted to go out and have fun, but it became painful for me and I was tired of struggling with Jocelyn everywhere we went. The many outfit changes, thinking she wasn't getting enough to eat because we were out in public… Our FAILURE of whatever we were doing wrong with her was now running our lives, effecting our marriage, and isolating us. The only answers we had received was FAILURE to thrive followed by developmental delay. I concluded that I had to get weight on her, so she could have the energy to crawl. I convinced myself that would fix things. Then she would walk soon after she started to crawl and then she could keep up with other kids like Jacob and McKenzie.

I decided to put Jocelyn and I in isolation, take matters into my own hands and tackle this head on! She could sit up now in her highchair and she could feed herself finger foods. No more baby food- she was almost a year- she needed fatty foods, which was recommended by a nutritionist we saw. Pancakes, fruit, sausage, french toast, biscuits and gravy. She grubbed down, feeding herself with both hands. Just shoveling it in. It was awesome. Sometimes, during the feed, she would "spit up" EVERYWHERE! Bath-for-the-baby, hose-for-the-highchair status. Super frustrating. I thought the answer to everything was nutrition. And despite extreme measures, in an instant, it would all come back out. I was so confused. Solid food is thicker, heavier… it should not come back free flowing as it always did. In my anatomy/physiology class I learned that the first part of the "gut" is the mouth and once you start to have teeth, that's the sign that the rest of the gut can also handle digesting food that needs to be chewed. Well, Baby Jo had 5 teeth and I was ready to try it- ready to fix this problem and help her!

One evening, after our meatless spaghetti dinner, it was straight to the bathtub with my happy messy girl. Tomato sauce was everywhere and I was so proud of her cuteness, she seemed so proud and happy of her full tummy and laughing with Mommy. It was fun. She grabbed her fishy bath toy and I started to undress her in the tub. *Uh oh*, I recognized the sound. The gates were opening and I was about to witness dinner- AGAIN. When she "spit up" I noticed something strange- sausage- perfectly rounded, undigested.

*What in the world?* I thought as I rinsed my 11 month olds mouth. *There was no sausage in the spaghetti?…* Then I remembered, Jocelyn had sausage for breakfast- 10 hours earlier! Why in the world does it look like she just ate it? "Delayed gastric emptying," to say the least!

I called her GI doctor and explained what had happened. He offered to restart "Medication XXX". "NO WAY!" I respectfully declined. However, we did agree to a barium swallow test with small bowel follow through. Being a nurse, I pretended to know what this was while talking to the doctor, then went straight to Google for all the details. Jocelyn would have to drink a bottle with barium (or dye) in it under an X-ray and they watch where the fluid goes. Then, a few hours later, repeat the X-ray to see how far the food or dye had gone. The sad part, the only opening for this procedure was on her actual birthday. Dennis and I decided we needed to know sooner, not later, what the results were. So we scheduled. We figured she was too young to know it was her birthday and we would just acknowledge her party as the big day.

The day of the procedure, Dennis had to work and I was alone to manage our one-year-old, who wasn't allowed to have anything to eat or drink prior to the procedure. I felt horrible, not providing for my child and her not understanding why. It broke my heart! Finally, in the x-ray room, I was able to give her a bottle (with dye in it) and she took it down the quickest I'd ever seen her take a bottle. This worried me because I knew a burp (with a "friend") was sure to come up. The technician advised me not to move her from laying down because there were "pictures" being taken of the dye traveling. What seemed like 30 minutes later, I was allowed to sit her up. Right as I sat her up, a large burp, with a large "friend" of spit up to accompany it landed all over the radiology table. Mortified, I apologized to the technician, gathered our belongings and ran out of the room. I sat in the waiting room and gave Jocelyn another bottle, knowing she was still hungry since most of the first bottle hadn't stayed down. The second bottle she sucked down slowly, enjoying every bit. After a small burp and a few small spit ups, we left the facility and took a cake to Daddy's work and celebrated her birthday for 20 minutes with him and his crew for the day.

A few days after the procedure, we received a letter in the mail explaining that results from the procedure were "normal".

We were pretty excited about making Jocelyn's first birthday a big celebration. We made it a whole year! We figured it would be soon now, without a doubt, that she would start walking. Then, it would increase her gastric emptying rate so she would stop spitting up too. We made it! I had it all planned out. It was time to celebrate! The party was over the top, indeed! We literally spent thousands and invited everyone we knew.

Jocelyn LOVED her dollies, "Babies". We called her "Baby Jo" all the time and we'd called her dolls "babies" so it was no wonder Jocelyn would call for them. "Be-Be" she would say, smile really big when you handed it to her, then she would quickly grab it with her hands, snuggle it in to her chest so tight and give that baby a big, wet, open mouth kiss. It was precious. So her birthday was a "Baby doll" themed birthday party. Hundreds of hand made invitations went out which included a cheesy poem I wrote:

> It's time to party
> Jocelyn is turning one,
> and she had an idea
> that will be so much fun!
> Those who know Jo
> Knows she loves her babies,
> so she wants you to bring your favorite
> to her first birthday party.

It was my best attempt at being a wholesome, "good" mother in this day and age's eyes. In a world where hand made stuff is a must, organic is the only way and a good mom breastfeeds for a year and only gives their children hand made baby food. There was no "keepin' up with the Jones'" here- I was trying to keep up with the rest of the world. I strived to be a "good" mom and, as medical charts already labeled, I was FAILING. The party was my opportunity to show the world that I was a good mom! I did love my daughter more than anything and would do anything for her- what better way does a mom show that than a BIG party?

Baby Jo sat in the middle of the room in her $60 white dress, what little peach fuz hair she had was curled thanks to the pokey "old lady" curlers. As guests began to arrive, she was completely content, wrestling with her favorite baby ensuring every inch of her was covered with wet kisses. One of Dennis' aunts arrived and brought her granddaughter, who is a few months younger than Jocelyn. The Aunt exclaimed to me attempting to give a compliment: "I can't believe how good Jocelyn is! She just sits there! She isn't getting into anything, she's just a good beautiful little girl!" I smiled politely, thanked her, and quickly left the room, pretending to do something. This was one of my fears about seeing everyone, especially those who hadn't seen much of us in the past year. It was her perception that Jocelyn was "good", the truth was, she was "delayed". I couldn't bring myself to correct her. The aunt's granddaughter, was literally, moving circles around Jocelyn. A site too unbearable to watch so I stirred the ranch dip 100 times to avoid witnessing this.

Jocelyn enjoyed her party, but seemed more confused at all the people and commotion than anything, which is to be expected of a one year old. My favorite part was her birthday cake. She had a "smash" cake placed in front of her while everyone sang to her. She watched the cake and looked curiously at it for a few minutes. Dennis had to finger a bite of frosting in her mouth so she could taste it and get interested. "MMmmmmm!" she nibbled on the frosting. Then she began to dig in! It was precious watching her feed herself and make a mess of her cake. A proud, happy moment for Dennis and I to enjoy. However, once I estimated that Jocelyn had enough cake to fill her tummy, I whisked her to the bathroom to clean her up before she spit up for the large audience of guests. I wanted them to remember how precious she was eating her cake and not remember poor Baby Jo tasting it twice!

When I took Jocelyn to the mall to get her 1 year pictures, I began to notice her starting to push on her upper abdomen- epigastric area. My heart broke as I thought she was in pain from the year long heartburn. I feared we would have to increase her acid reducer medication. *If only she'd walk...* I daydreamed. But then, she started pushing on her "diaper" area too. I thought maybe she wasn't keeping enough water down so she was getting a bladder infection due to dehydration. My nurse mind would spin and spin and spin, then my mommy reaction was striving to fix things ASAP! Dennis could see my reaction to everything and perceived it as extreme. "She's fine" he'd attempt to console me. I saw his response as resistance and ignorance. We just had her first birthday- things were supposed to be on the up and up. Not more problems, but less. Not more bickering from Dennis and I about what to do/what not to do, but a time to move on with life and enjoy our daughter and family.

Things definitely did not resolve after her first birthday. They rapidly got worse. I took her to the doctor for the pushing on her epigastric area, alternating with her "diaper" area.

"Everything is normal." We were sent home. "Continue with occupational therapy and she is still under weight on the growth chart so 'FAILURE to thrive' remains on the chart."

"Awesome" I sarcastically said as we left the doctor. *I might not be a doctor, but I am her mom and this is not NORMAL*, I thought to myself.

About a month after the epigastric and diaper pushing it suddenly stopped. Just like that, over night- done. But then something came on more aggressive than the tummy/diaper pushing... hand mouthing! It was crazy how far she would stick her hands in her mouth, sometimes making herself gag. When we had play time on the carpet with toys all around, she started to ignore them. Her favorite fishy toys and dancing light up bears went unnoticed. She just looked at them with her hands in her mouth. Then it progressed during breakfast in her highchair. She'd just stare at her food and cried and put her hands in her mouth.

I took her to the dentist with my wild nurse imagination. *Maybe she has an infected molar growing in. An abscess... something... I've seen a lot of weird stuff roll through the ER... there has to be something we are missing.* The dentist said the molars were there, but not quiet close to cutting the gum line. He then looked at me, put an apologetic hand on my shoulder and said, "You have a beautiful daughter" and then walked away. *What the heck was that for?* I thought. *Don't pity us, help us!* I demanded in my head. Irritated, we went home.

The struggle continued for weeks. She sat in her chair and cried with her hands in her mouth. I'm a tough love kind of parent and I knew she could feed herself. She had done it for months. I would get so mad at Dennis when he would give in and spoon feed her.

"You're spoiling her," I warned him. Then he would get out more and more bottles. I was so disgusted. We were trying to wean her from the bottle and go to only sippy cups. She had used cups for months. *Why is he going backwards and undoing all the work we have done over the last few months?* The marriage battle continued as we both thought we were doing what was right for our Baby Jo.

But then it wasn't just breakfast she wouldn't eat. Then it was lunch too. She would cry and cry and cry and put her hands in her mouth. I refused to give in! Early terrible 2's or something! Maybe she's mad she can't crawl or walk yet. At one point my mom pointed out she stopped saying "mom" and "dog" and "dada" and "hi". "Yes, she still does!" I argued.

Looking back now I think I was so concerned with her not eating that I hadn't noticed she didn't call for me much anymore. I needed her to eat! That would fix things! Nutrition is so important, especially the first 5 years. That's what all the books said. She needs energy! To gain some weight!

One stubborn morning, I was determined for Jocelyn to feed herself. In her highchair, I put in front of her some of her favorites. Cinnamon toast, diced peaches and egg. She swatted at a few items but nothing made it to her mouth. My frustration burned my cheeks. I calmly cleared the try and gave her round two of breakfast. Pancakes and watermelon. Again, she swatted at a few items and the only thing that made it into her mouth was her hands. I was determined for her to feed herself! I sat and waited and watched. Jocelyn began to get upset, which only fueled my frustration. I got out the video camera and documented this event. Every doctor visit, they told me everything was "normal". Well, I wanted the doctors to witness first hand how not "normal" this was. I documented, experimented with different food. I strived to find a solution. I was separating myself. I was the researcher and Jocelyn was my subject.

After over an hour of my experiment, I gave in to my frustration. I took off my researcher hat and was a confused mom again. Jocelyn's tears and screaming of frustration literally got under my skin. I was red from head to toe with boiling blood. I got her out off her chair, took her to my bedroom and I stood her up leaning with her back against my bed to support her and sat down in front of her. Eye to eye. I begged her "STOP IT JOCELYN! WHY WONT YOU EAT! YOU HAVE TO EAT! STOP

PUTTING YOUR HANDS IN YOUR MOUTH! YOUR TEETH ARE FINE! EVERYBODY GROWS TEETH!"

Jocelyn started to get her precious lip out! The adorable bottom lip that tucked under to give a warning to a tear coming soon! My begging turned into a bawling blubbering cry: "WHAT'S WRONG WITH YOU? YOU WONT EVEN TRY! I KNOW YOU CAN FEED YOURSELF! YOU'VE DONE IT FOR MONTHS! WHY ARE YOU DOING THIS?"

At that moment, Jocelyn began to cry and vigorously shook her head "NO NO NO NO" as if she were telling me: "you've got it all wrong, Mom, STOP!" At that moment, I stopped crying and I was so proud that she communicated. She told me "NO!" I got through to her, but more importantly, SHE got through to ME! I could see it in her eyes. The last thing she wanted to do was disappoint me. I wiped my tears and hers, swallowed my pride, made her another lunch and spoon fed it to her- AND SHE ATE IT! This was the moment my quest began. Something beyond my daughter's control was overcoming her- and it infuriated me! I was no longer "tough loving" her- I then knew, she wanted help! She was trying to figure out too, what was wrong. Her "NO NO NO" of her head vigorously shaking was my wake up call and her desperate cry for help. This was no longer "her against me". I was in this with her and I was going to love her through it and be there every heart beat of the way!

The next few months were busy to say the least. I was on a mission! Something was wrong with my baby and I needed help. Throughout this part of the journey, there were so many opinions flying around from friends, family, and co-workers:

"She's fine, she will walk."

"All these tests procedures and everything keeps coming back normal- you act like you WANT something wrong with her."

"When is enough enough, Beth?"

I didn't care, I didn't listen. I knew something was wrong and I was tired of denial and pride. I would no longer rest in the reassurance of others who had no clue what was going on in our house day in and day out. Not to mention- I AM HER MOTHER! I knew something wasn't right.

I didn't care what others thought, I cared what Jocelyn thought. I wasn't going to roll over and ignore the fact that she was slipping farther and farther away! I had to act, no matter who was with or against me. I knew this was going to have to be my war- I couldn't ask anyone else to drive Jocelyn to the multitude of therapies and specialists- all at least an hour away. Dennis and I agreed that I needed to take time off work to figure things out.

I had 8 weeks, ready… GO!

During one of many blood draws, ordered by one of many of Jocelyn's specialist referrals, my eyes were opened like never before. Jocelyn was a beautiful little one year old, sitting on my lap quietly looking around at the blood draw station. The middle aged woman phlebotomist glanced through the orders while commenting on how pretty Jocelyn was.

"What a beautiful little girl. Why in the world is she getting her blood drawn for all of these silly tests. These doctors are just really over doing it."

I sat in silence with my head hung low with guilt. As she tied the tourniquet around my daughter's tiny arm, I started to question myself as her opinion continued.

"Why can't people just let kids be kids. Absolutely ridiculous!" she continued. "All this blood, all these tests, just so sad what they are doing to our children, don't you think?" she looked at me, looking for approval. I ignored her question when I noticed all the vials.

"Are those pediatric tubes?" I demanded.

"No, we don't have any pediatric size in this lab," she replied with sass.

"Then, I hope you aren't filling all of them all the way up!" I argued.

"Well I have to for the amount of tests they ordered" she rebutted. I looked at the table of tubes filled with Jocelyn's blood as she was pulling the needle out of quiet Jocelyn. *One, two, three, four... SEVEN! SEVEN vials out of my one year old, filled up!* I snapped out of my guilt trance which this lady put me in and looked at Jo. Her head was bobbing and she appeared to be fighting sleep- right after a needle was in her arm. Most one year olds are still crying from being traumatized about the needle. I tried so hard not to panic.

"Ohhhhh" the phlebotomist looked at Jocelyn in awe of her beauty, "it must be nap time" she ignorantly commented, clueless to the fact that she could have induced this sudden fatigue. "Make sure you give her extra water today, and maybe even some juice."

I ignored her, swooped up my things and my limp daughter and went to the car. I tantrumed in my head all the way to the car, *I can't give her extra fluid, or orange juice, Lady! That is the problem! That's a huge reason for all these 'ridiculous' tests*"! I was so mad at myself. Instead of keeping focus on Jocelyn, I sat and listened to that woman's judgement: "ridiculous", "unnecessary", "silly", "over doing it"... I called Dennis at work from my truck, trying not to panic. I did the best assessment I could on sleeping Jocelyn in the back of the truck. She wasn't due for a nap for another 2 hours and I couldn't fully wake her up! Her skin looked good, her pulses were strong and regular... I reported my assessment findings to Dennis and he calmly, as always, gave reassurance, "Just take her home, Beth, and take it easy today. No therapy! Just relax. I'm sure she is fine. That phlebotomist is an idiot, you didn't do anything wrong..."

It took Jocelyn a good week to regain all her strength. Within that time frame, I pulled out my pediatric nursing books and did some calculations as to how much blood loss she had based on her weight and filling all of the vials full of blood: 20% blood volume loss! At 25% loss, it is protocol to start transfusion and begin resuscitation measures. I carried the guilt, not for the labels the stranger put on me, but of trusting someone caring for my daughter without paying close attention. From there on out, I demanded to be informed of every little detail and I watched like a hawk, everyone. A new label came about that I could hear the nurses and staff warn each other: "OH, AND MOM'S A NURSE." Being a nurse, I knew exactly what that meant. A pain in the butt family member, wanting to be involved in the care. "YEP," I accepted this label every time, "Be warned people! I learned my lesson and I am watching you! That will NEVER happen again."

Here's a list of Jocelyn's scheduled appointments and tests starting from when our quest began.

4-24-09 : blood work ordered by primary doctor: phosphorus, magnesium calcium, complete blood count, urinalysis, fecal glob in, prealbumin, total protein, alkaline phosphates, amylase, gamma glutamyl transferase, lactate dehydrogenase, alanine aminotransferase, aspartate aminotransferase, eletrolytes, blood urea nitrogen, creatinine ALL WITHIN NORMAL LIMITS

4-27-09 barrium swallow test with small bowel follow through

5-1-09 GI doctor

5-22-09 primary doctor- "rash"- Jocelyn was scratching everywhere

5-22-09 GI doctor

5-26-09 Nutritionist

6-8-09 GI doctor

6-8-09 Occupational Therapy session

6-17-09 First opinion neurologist

6-29-09 GI doctor

7-7-09 Occupational Therapy session

7-15-09 primary doctor, asking for referral for second opinion neurologist

7-24-09 geneticists evaluation

7-28-09 Occupational Therapy session

7-29-09 GI doctor

7-30-09 Physical Therapy Evaluation

8-4-09 Second opinion neurologist ordered labs: pyruvate, ammonia, creatine kinase, thyroid stimulating hormone, uric acid, calcium.

8-5-09 endocrinologist who ordereD labs: ionized calcium level, phosphorus, total protein, parathyroid hormone, magnesium.

8-11-09 Occupational Therapy session

8-11-09 endocrinologist ordered labs: alkaline phosphatase, magnesium, phosphorus, calcium, ionized calcium

8-20-09 Physical Therapy session

8-24-09 primary doctor visit for Jocelyn hitting herself in the head and pulling her hair

8-26-09 Occupational Therapy session

9-1-09 Ophthalmologist- had to leave because Jocelyn screamed the whole time

9-4-09 MRI of head while being intubated and sedated

9-6-09 Catscan of head

9-14-09 GI doctor: ordered Fecal Globin

9-14-09 Physical Therapy session

9-16-09 Occupational Therapy session

10-13-09 back to first opinion neurologist

10-13-09 Occupational Therapy session

11-3-09 Occupational Therapy session

11-6-09 Orthopedics- X-rays of hips and spine and legs to see why she's not walking

11-6-09 Ophthalmologist- round two

11-9-09 geneticist- Angelman's test ordered

11-9-09 GI doctor

11-12-09 Upper endoscopy with biopsy- NORMAL

11-19-09 primary doctor ordered labs: electrolytes, calcium, blood urea nitrogen, creatinine

11-24-09 Occupational Therapy test

12-8-09 Occupational Therapy test

12-8-09 hearing test

12-23-09 repeat hearing test

1-18-10 neurologist ordered labs: rett test, lead

1-27-10 primary doctor appointment for clearance for sedative hearing test

2-9-10 sedative hearing test

2-9-10 D day

## The Drawing Board

Finally- a possible answer on a blood draw early August. Her calcium was low! Jocelyn's was 7 and normal is 8.5-10.7. I did my research and found that low calcium can cause muscle cramps, spasms, and twitching and tingling in the fingers and around the mouth! I felt so reassured. My suspicions of all of this drama being diet related had just been confirmed! It made sense: her legs would sometimes stiffen up (muscle spasms), her hands and mouth felt funny so she'd put her hands in her mouth! I just knew this was it! All I had to do was give her more Calcium or a supplement! *Oh Baby Girl! We're going to fix this!*

One week later, my spirits were crushed. During a referral to the endocrinologist we learned that the supportive blood tests for low calcium were not suggestive of Jocelyn having low calcium. He believed the results to be a false positive. Just in case, he ordered repeat blood tests 2 weeks after initial blood draw. He was right. The false low calcium was a fluke! Back to the drawing board...

Our second opinion neurologist suggested an MRI of Jocelyn's brain to look at it's structure. She explained that MRI's take up to 45 minutes of the patient holding completely still. Such a task for a 1 year old was impossible, therefore it required to medically paralyze and sedate her during the test. The thought terrified Dennis and I. The thought of our little girl being intubated was horrifying. I hated medications, especially how "neuro" Jocelyn seemed to me: eye rolling when getting excited and about to laugh, stiffening of legs when excited or being vocal, not walking, hand mouthing, looking lost, I had even described her as looking Autistic… Consenting to medication for sedation which would mess with the nervous system nauseated me. My biggest fear was that they wouldn't be able to remove her from the ventilator- I've seen it happen at work- a simple procedure then "something happens".

The procedure was to be done in Los Angeles so we stayed at Dennis' parents house at the beach- a 45 minute drive versus a 2 and a half hour drive from our home. My doubt and worry about whether I was doing the right thing silently haunted me. I was making such huge decisions for my child and she was so vulnerable and trusting. Filled with doubt, it could've been my imagination, but I felt the tense presence of resentment towards me everywhere I turned.

The night before the test, I was upstairs packing the diaper bag, I heard Dennis take a call from his sister in Arizona then disappear outside. I could hear him from an opened window telling her, "Just another stinkin' test, I'm sure it'll come back normal, just like all the rest of them." I wanted to vomit! When I heard him get off the phone I met him outside in a rage.

"What in the world is your problem?! If you are so confident that nothing is wrong with her, why did you consent to this? Do you think I want to see Jocelyn go through this? Or that I would put her through this if I thought everything was fine? You think I want something wrong with her?!"

He raged back "I think everything will be fine! Yes, I want this test done, so we know everything is fine! I was just telling my sister not to worry!"

There could've been unicorns running down the street as we argued and we would've never heard them or noticed. I was playing defense- it was me against everyone, against the world! For so many weeks Jocelyn and I saw doctor after doctor after doctor without any success for answers. Just more and more hoops to jump and fight through. In this moment, I suddenly felt my husband changed his position from my offense to defense. I let him have every ounce of built up rage over the past few weeks. It was really me against the world and especially, me against this driving force that was kidnapping my daughter, slowly, everyday, right before my eyes. It didn't matter to me if I was FAILING yet again. I wasn't going to waver or back down. Failure to diagnose was not going to happen. I would've fought anything and anyone, however long it took to get my daughter back. I'd even fight my husband. What an easy target for me too, he was always right there... We unleashed on each other for a good hour before going our separate ways to bed, in silence.

The next morning came. Pre procedure was the hardest, Jocelyn being hungry wanting her bottle and we couldn't comply. She didn't understand. All she knew was that her needs weren't being met and Mommy and Daddy were both right there, not providing! Horrid feeling. We got to hold her when the anesthesiologist gave her a little bit of oral sedation and she soon acted drunk. Dennis and I somewhat smiled at each other- the first time we had acknowledged each other's existence in 18 hours. We watched together our sleepy little girl and how peaceful she became as her hands left her mouth and she just stared deeply at us, in love. We each kissed her head one last time, then left our baby behind with the procedure team.

Then we waited. And waited. Dennis and I spoke little during our wait.

"Want food?"

"Sure". It wasn't that we were hungry, it just seemed like that's what we were supposed to do. It was something to do, to keep us busy and our minds off the fact that our hungry baby was at the mercy of someone else. The white elephant went with us to every waiting area we found. Not exactly speaking to Dennis, my thoughts wandered to the day Jocelyn was born, my first bout of separation anxiety when she was just a few minutes old and they took her to the recovery room before I got to go. I decided this separation anxiety was most nauseatingly worse!

Finally, 90 minutes after we last saw our little girl, we were called to the recovery room. I could see her in a crib across the room and I wanted to run to it. There she was, looking so tiny in the giant metal crib, snoozing with her legs and arms spread like a starfish as she always did. I was so relieved she had an IV going- *At least she is getting fluid and a little bit of sugar and electrolytes,* I thought, still feeling guilty for not feeding her that morning. Dennis pet her head lovingly and softly as she slept. I was still defensively irritated with him, but seeing his love for her melted my heart. I couldn't stand to see him hurt over his tortured daughter. Two hours later, Jocelyn finally woke up and we soothed her coarse voice from intubation with some cherry jello. We were sent home a few hours later and were told we'd have results in a few days during a follow up appointment. We returned to Dennis' parents house, in attempts to make a mini vacation out of this horrible experience and take Jocelyn to the beach when she was feeling up for it.

The next day, as we were about to feed Jocelyn lunch and feast on some of Sally's awesome guacamole, my cell phone beeped with a message. The voicemail was a man with a thick indistinguishable accent. What I could understand on the message was that the MRI showed that Jocelyn may have a blockage in one of her main arteries to her brain and we needed to come back to the ER immediately. I screamed for Dennis in confusion as I ran upstairs to pack all of our stuff. He followed me upstairs trying to figure out what was wrong, why I was screaming. In a nervous panic, barely able to catch my breath, I explained in 2 word sentences to Dennis what the doctor said. Dennis finally just listened to the message himself to figure out what I was trying to say. Dennis shot back downstairs to get Jocelyn ready and to tell his parents. I was shaking so bad I could barely zip my duffle bag. *This is why she was punching herself in the head the past few weeks*, I thought, terrified but relieved to have answers! *My poor girl has had a headache and has been trying to tell me!*

Then my medical reasoning brought doubt to my thoughts, *Why was she able to move both sides of her body equally strong? Why weren't her pupils unequal? How long could she have really lived like this- her symptoms started months ago?*

I quickly disregarded these thoughts and went to more positive medical thoughts: *So will they be able to evacuate the blockage with some guided wire like they do in the cardiac cathlab at work? I wonder what recovery time is? How much longer can I be off work? I wonder if she will start walking right away or will it take a month or so?*

I hopped in the car, Jocelyn was already buckled in and my phone rang again:

"Hello?"

"Mrs. Jones, this is Dr Neuro at the hospital. You need to bring Jocelyn here immediately and I will meet you in the ER."

"Yes, we are in the car, on our way. It's about a 45 min drive. We will be there as soon as I can."

Dennis went back in the house to be sick before backing out. Sally, helpless, worried, not knowing how to help tried handing me $100. "We're fine Sally, thank you. We will call you when we know more."

We arrived at the ER and everyone was expecting us like we were VIP at a club. The three of us we were immediately taken back to a room. When this happened in the ER I worked at, it usually means big business and something pretty serious. Acute- something suddenly wrong. I was confused as to why Jocelyn was so emergent, why had been so stable for months and now emergent. I just went with the flow, did what we were told, but couldn't help but wonder what the next 12 hours looked like.

The neurologist came in and explained that on the MRI, they couldn't see blood flow from the vessel that feeds the back of the brain. The only way to determine there is a blockage is a CAT scan with dye. "Okay," Dennis and I both agreed.

"If there is a blockage, we will talk after the CAT scan as to what the next step is" the doctor continued.

"Okay," Dennis and I said in sequence. "Do we have to sedate her for the CAT scan?" I asked.

"No, just make her fall asleep or you can hold her still."

After an hour of trying to put her to sleep, I couldn't take not knowing if my child's brain wasn't getting blood any more. I called for the nurse. "Let's do this," I told him. The nurse called the radiology department and we took her down. We attempted to help Jocelyn hold still, but she was tired, hungry, and probably scared. I eagerly agreed to the staff taping her to a back board in order to have her hold still so they could get the 1 minute test finished with. It was teeth clenching horrible hearing her cry because she was restrained, but it was only for a short time. Right when it was finished, still taped to the board, I recognized a horrifying sound.

"ROLL HER! SHE'S GOING TO VOMIT!" I screamed from behind a glass wall. Taped to the board, they flipped Baby Jo on her side and she spit up everywhere. The nurse suctioned her to prevent the stomach contents going into her lungs while the radiology tech cut her free from the board. Dennis and I ran in and cleaned her up. She was scared and shaking, but okay. My blood filled quickly with anger. *Can't she catch a break?!* I scorned the universe silently. I held her tight and she fell asleep, exhausted from all the commotion. We went back to our camp in the ER room and waited.

An hour later the neurologist came in, "Okay, you can go home!" he announced proudly. I nodded my head at him, as if I was understanding what he was saying, but really I was trying to digest what just happened the last 6 hours. The doctor continued, "The MRI was just artifact- a fuzzy part so we couldn't see the blood flow. The CT looks great. Everything is normal." Then he left the room. Dennis and I packed up in silence.

It wasn't that I wanted Jocelyn to have a blockage or have a brain procedure, or anything serious and emergent like that, I just thought we had an answer. If we had found a problem, we could find a direction to take to fix it. The car ride home was filled with text messages from friends and family who had heard the good news from our mothers that everything was good and we were on our way back to the beach. Yes, good news. But my daydream of her walking in a month, calling me Mom in a few days, playing with her toys again… all of it was thrown out the window on the 101 freeway. Back to the drawing board.

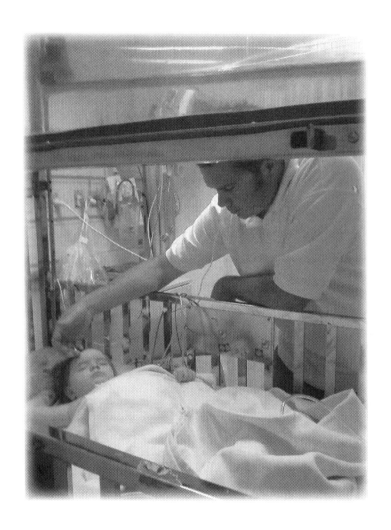

During the year of Jocelyn being one while we journeyed all over Southern California looking for answers, I felt her slipping further and further away from me. The hand mouthing became more obsessive, eye contact was limited, her food sat on her plate untouched, her toys on the ground right next to her, remained lonely. If we picked her up, she would snuggle and fall asleep. This only fueled me to go faster to find out what was going on with her.

When we were referred to a new specialist, the mornings of those appointments there was a sense of hope and excitement of the possibilities of answers. I'd top Jocelyn off with a bottle then put her in the car naked, surrounded by towels. Not 5 minutes down the road I could hear her spit up. We'd drive for an hour and show up in the parking structure 30 minutes early so I could clean her up, get out her stroller and sign in. When the nurse would get vital signs and engage with us, every time, right on cue they'd ask "Ohhhh, is she teething?" as they watched Baby Jo vigorously shoving both hands down her throat.

"Yep," I'd reply shortly, attempting to make it obvious that I didn't want to talk about it.

"And why are you seeing Doctor today?" they'd routinely ask.

"Referral" I'd bark back. Sometimes Jocelyn would start to act out, screaming, pulling her hair with her right hand and punching her head with her left, as she had been doing for weeks. Then I'd sarcastically point to her as if she was the answer. "And THAT!"

"Ohhhh, what's wrong with her?" the nurse would baby talk concerned.

"That's the million dollar question. Which room would you like us in?" I'd defensively snap because I just wanted to hide in a room before her tantrum got worse. I wasn't there to talk to the nurse. I wanted the specialist that might have the answer for the million dollar question. I was focused, gloves laced up, ready to fight if I had to, ready to get to the bottom of all this!

When the specialist of the week would come in we'd start with an interview of questions starting from pregnancy. Eventually, the repetitive interviews began to feel like an interrogation on me:

"How was your pregnancy? Any complication?"

"Preterm labor at 24 weeks."

"Well, were you working?"

"Yes."

"I see... What do you do?"

"I'm on my feet a lot." I avoided as best I could to volunteer information that I was a RN. I didn't want the doctors to expect me to know something when maybe I didn't.

"Did you drink during your pregnancy?"

"No."

"Any drugs during pregnancy?"

"No."

"Did you smoke during your pregnancy?"

"No."

"Do you or anyone smoke around the baby now?"

"No."

"Did you travel out of the country while pregnant?"

"Yes, we went to Mexico and stayed at a resort" I'd admit.

"I see... Have you ever had an STD?"

"No."

"Did you deliver full term?"

"41 weeks."

"C-section? Why?!... oh, I see..."

"Did you breastfeed"

"Yes."

"For how long?"

"3 months."

"Did you vaccinate Jocelyn?"...

With every new doctor the same interrogation. Looking for a reason for a sick kid can kill a parent! I held it together every visit. I would absolutely take punches and accusations a thousand times over if one of these doctors would finally get to the bottom of what did go wrong! Constant interrogation helped me position myself more firmly on defense. It was me against the next guy, and for Jocelyn, I put myself through it.

Then the doctor would interact with Jocelyn, do a physical assessment, then order any tests they thought might help. It was always "I'm not sure but we can look at [X,Y, Z], but I have a feeling they will come back normal. Maybe you should follow up with [such and such] specialty next." Then they'd point the finger in a new direction of where I should go and I'd comply. The process would repeat over and over and over...

Going home with Jocelyn after each appointment answerless, we would both feel tired and defeated. Whatever hope I had that morning would drift away. When we got home I would calorie count Jocelyn's intake for the day and realize we would come up short. I was frustrated that time in the car could have been time giving her a snack or staying on some sort of schedule. So now my "failure to thrive" baby was missing meals as I was trying to find out WHY she is failure to thrive. An absolute catch 22 and with every decision I made Jocelyn had to face the consequences.

A day with a doctor appointment, Jocelyn was usually so tired she wouldn't tolerate to stay up late and catch up on calories. She would go to bed so early and it frustrated me. I would always complain how 5pm bedtimes are not normal for a one year old. "She needs it" Dennis would reassure me. I would be torn and alone when she went to bed and Dennis was at work. Hopeful at morning, defeated, clueless and on defense by dinner. I would self medicate with a six pack of beer, trying to numb my emotional day. I felt trapped. Worried. Helpless. Hopeless. Alone...

When I wasn't alone, when Dennis was off and we'd come home from a doctor's appointment, we'd usually find him cooking dinner for us, drinking a beer, rocking out to Jimmy Buffet or something. I would be emotionally drained, frustrated with Jocelyn's screaming all day. Dennis irritated me that he was enjoying himself. Some nights, I'd hand over Jocelyn, give him report as if he was a fellow nurse taking over patient care "She last ate this much at this time, went poop yesterday, 3 1 hour naps today and she's ready for bed" I'd snap then go lock myself in the closet, lay on the floor and cry. If I felt alone, that's exactly what I wanted to be- by choice though! Alone in a dark closet!

Oh the disagreements this would lead to. We both loved our Baby Jo, we just didn't know how to deal with everything together. He would try and be nonchalant, I would be worried, scrambling and just "doing". I remember thinking that I was living a statistic. We were the parents of a sick kid and the divorce rate is very high in those situations and our fighting was a red flag. We knew we loved each other. We knew we loved Jo. We just couldn't figure out how to live and help her at the same time.

*No body gets it* laying on the dark closet floor my mind wondered. *No one knows, Dennis is out there irritated with me, playing with Jocelyn, and I am laying on the floor of our closet at the end of my rope. Everyone else in the world is going about their daily lives. Kids having playdates, going to the park... I spent all day, all WEEK at doctor's offices with my screaming, probably starving child!*

The urgency to scream at the top of my lungs was too much to contain. I didn't just want to shout, I wanted to scream! At the top of mountain tops! "THIS IS CRAZY! LOOK AT THIS! MY FAMILY IS FALLING APART!!" No one knew and I wanted to tell everyone! I wanted help! I had no clue how anyone else could help, but I just knew I needed help! For the first time since we began our journey to find out what was wrong with Baby Jo, I didn't want to fight the world, I wanted to share! I wanted to scream at the top of my lungs on a mountain so every soul could hear my cries, listen to what a chaotic mess my life had become. I had been in isolation for so long now, no one probably even noticed I was gone, out of the loop. I felt like no one even noticed what my family was going through!

*A book! I could write a book right now with everything our family has been through!* I thought my idea was genius. Maybe if I were more detailed in describing what had been taking place, someone who read my book would help me figure out what was going on with my Baby Jo. Laura suddenly came to mind, her husband just got his bachelor's in English and someone told me he was a writer. With my eyes blood shot with tears I could barely see what I was texting Laura:

"Hey girl, it's Beth Jones. I want to write a book, do you think Eric would help me?"

A few minutes of laying in silence in my dark closet, my phone lit up the small room with Laura's reply, "Ummmm, sure, lol. I'm sure he would, you'd just have to ask him."

I suddenly realized how confused she must have been. I hadn't seen her or talked to her in months. She didn't know my day to day that we were living, how Jocelyn had gotten worse, every single day! We rarely talked I was honestly shocked the number I had for her still worked. Embarrassment filled my already red face. *How stupid am I? She has no clue what's going on over here because I put our family on lock down. I can't write a book… I'm a science major. I've always struggled with English… "LOL" is right.* The idea left as quickly as it came.

Going back to work was a break from all the drama at home. It was my time for adult interaction, with my co-workers. I was "Beth", not the crazy mom who insisted something was wrong with her precious daughter. Emergency medicine was paradise compared to what I was dealing with in my four walls. It was instant gratification giving answers for patients with a few simple tests: "you're having a heart attack, this is what we need to do", "you broke your foot, you need a cast", "it's an appendicitis, we are calling the operating room staff"… Problem- tests- diagnosis- SOLUTION! AMAZING! Not at all what I was experiencing with Jocelyn. At home we had hours and hours and hours of in home therapy interrupting our lives every single day. And seeing little progress over a long period of time. Every specialist was a list of tests and blood draws with no answers… Two completely different realms of care, and I was ready for the one that gave instant satisfaction. I needed that sense of value not FAILURE. I was making a difference at work, I was helping people! At home, I felt I wasn't helping my daughter, at all.

I had a wonderful support system at work. The ER doctors- I trusted. The fellow nurses- had my back. I loved the technicians, my supervisors, and other ancillary services within the hospital. Everyone would ask how Jocelyn was doing, if she made any progress or if we found any answers for a diagnosis yet. A simple, "She's good", "We're fine", and "No, not yet" were my routine answers, with body language not inviting further conversation about it.

When I came back, something seemed different though. My perspective had changed on so many things. Perhaps it was my experience being on the other end of the healthcare system. Without knowing exactly what was going on with Jocelyn, I knew at any moment, she could quickly be a patient again. It frightened me, but I became more sensitive to what patients and family members were going through or how they might want to be treated.

One day, in particular, I remember we were extremely busy and an ambulance was bringing in a 8 year old girl from school, having a seizure. She had a history of seizures and by the time she got to the ER, she was done with her seizure and awake. She did not speak but looked frightened as I watched the paramedic give the doctor and 2 nurses report at bedside while the doctor was assessing her. She didn't fight, she didn't cry, she just sat calm, watching everything unfold around her. My co-workers were focused on the medical- the vitals- looking to find the problem so they could fix it. I, on the other hand, watched her eyes. The doctor told the nurses what he was going to order as he left the bedside and the 2 nurses started to get to work, undressing the 8 year old and getting her in a gown.

I cut in front of them and looked her in her eyes, "Hi there! My name is Beth and I am a nurse and I'm going to help you. You had a seizure at school today." The little girl looked deep into my eyes, focusing on every word I spoke. Jocelyn looked at me the same way- I knew the little girl understood.

"Teacher said she doesn't talk" the paramedic yelled from the other side of the curtain.

"Thank you" I politely disregarded him.

"Does anything hurt?"

The little girl shook her head "Yes."

"Does your head hurt?"

Again, she shook her head "Yes."

"Does anything else hurt?"

She shook her head "No".

"Does your head always hurt when you have a seizure?"

"Yes" the head nod.

"Did you hit your head today?"

"No" with her head nod.

"Okay, we will give you some medicine so your head wont hurt anymore. Your teacher called your mom and she's coming in. For now, I'm going to help you get in this hospital dress. Then were going to get some pee when you have to go potty. The doctor also wants a blood test, okay?"

One tear rolled down her adorable full cheek as she shook her head "yes".

My co-workers looked over at me and complemented "Your good with her, I think she likes you."

I fought back tears as hard as I could.

And then I broke.

I turned quickly in hopes the little scared patient couldn't see. I went outside to the ambulance bay to get some fresh air and to privately collect myself. What if that happened to Jocelyn? She seemed so "neuro" to me, and I feared that one day she, too, would have a seizure. One day soon, Jocelyn would be going to school. I feared that she would be in this little patient's place: having a seizure at school with mom not readily available to meet her at the hospital. My heart broke for the patient, for her mother. My heart broke for my future, again, staring me in the face, now at work even- my safe haven. I couldn't break away from it. I've changed. This is the new "me" and I could not escape.

With my new eyes and my new perspective, I could see the nurse I used to be in my co-workers. There was always a rationale for every horrible thing we would see. Someone to blame. It was safer that way- if we knew what not to do, then it wouldn't happen to us. For example:

* An infant CPR, suspected sudden infant death syndrome (SIDS)- Nurses will discreetly interrogate the paramedics for information, looking for risk factors to SIDS: Did the house smell like smoke?

Was the baby sleeping on its back? Was there adequate circulation in the room where the baby was sleeping? Quizzing like vultures to see which of the risk factor this poor little life had had which resulted in SIDS. If there was a preventable cause for this tragic event, then there was a sense of security in the nurses that it wouldn't happen to their babies.

* Near drowning accident. Who was with the child? How did this happen? Were any adults around?
* 40 year old CPR. Did they smoke? They're a little over weight. Are they diabetic? Are their parents still alive? Any siblings die at an early age? Maybe it's a genetic thing...

When nurses act like this, my old self included, it is not because we think we are detectives or that we are playing the blame game to judge people in their horrible circumstances. The fact of the matter is, it is a coping mechanism. We see first hand how short life can be; how one wrong choice can be fatal. ER nurses see the worst of the worst situations and continuously come back to work the next day. If they are able to find reason in the tragedy, they understand how to protect themselves and their loved ones from that tragedy happening to them. How else could we leave our families and go to work the next day? If we embrace the fact that anything can happen to anyone at any given point and we are not in control, we would sit at home holding onto our families, in fear, that they could be next. A critical care nurse feeling lack of control is not a happy camper!

So what about Jocelyn? What about me? With every specialist, every doctor, every assessment/interrogation, no one could ever find anything that Dennis and I did wrong to have a special needs child.

# The Mother Daughter Dance

At 16 months old, Jocelyn's occupational therapist explained that Jocelyn wasn't gaining skills as planned, so she wanted to go from sessions twice a week to once a month.

*WHAT?!*

This made no sense to me. I tried to relate in terms I understood- Nursing. So, if my patient wasn't responding well to whatever treatment we were using, I sit back and take a longer lunch? NO! I upgrade to the Intensive Care Unit and get more aggressive treatment going. I was so offended that this OT was giving up on my baby!

During this same time, we started physical therapy. Our therapist, during our first evaluation expressed concern, and was very straight forward with us. "Ummm, she is pretty delayed- this is more long term care versus what insurance will pay for. Are you receiving services through IRC?"

"Is that the 'Inland' thing that just started sending a teacher to the house? I thought that was all they could help us with," I replied confused.

"Yes, Inland Regional Center. Insurance will cover therapies for acute care. Jocelyn is going to need long term therapy. That's what IRC covers- state funded programs."

Surprisingly, I wasn't at all offended that she was so confident that my child needed long term therapy- I was so appreciative of her honesty. She was not the help that Jocelyn needed.

"Well how do I do that?" And so it began, our journey into "THE SYSTEM". *Whatever-* we needed help!

Insurance stopped Jocelyn's therapy once we started to pursue IRC.

It took months to get approved and the wait times for assessments was ridiculous. My appreciation for our insurance grew during this time.

It was an oxymoron to cal "the system" a system at all.

I politely waited for answers and for people to return my calls- it was like pulling teeth. Finally, enough was enough. I began to call Jocelyn's case worker for IRC daily. After a week, she finally returned my call. She explained that what was taking so long was that we didn't have a diagnosis. I was working on that, obviously, by my list of activities during that time. This was what she instructed me to do, without question: "Go to your doctor. Have him write on a piece of prescription paper 'diagnosis: Cerebral Palsy.' Then bring it to my office".

"I am not telling a doctor what to diagnose my daughter with. Especially when I know that this isn't Cerebral Palsy. Jocelyn wasn't like this since birth. Something changed! SOMETHING IS WRONG!" I explained to her. This was a turning point in my mission to get Jocelyn help- no longer was I trusting the system or anyone. This was not how I worked. My daughter deserved better than this!

"Well then I can't help you. If you won't do that then you'll have to wait," and she hung up on me.

*What in the world is this? The DMV? The twilight zone? What kind of human works in a position as a case worker who has no heart or compassion!* I cried and cried in frustration, but not defeat! Time to press harder!

I spoke to a supervisor, then a manager, then an "after hours" supervisor. I called every day until I got answers and time frames as to when Jocelyn could have therapy again. My daughter was slipping away further and further during this time and I was in a panic as to whether I made the wrong decision to pursue IRC versus just sticking with once a month occupational therapy through insurance. Guilt, pressure, doubt... I became a ball of emotions as I watched the evidence of my decisions right in front of my face, slipping through my fingers.

What IRC was providing us with was a "pediatric care specialist" every Monday morning from 8-10. We were nervous to have someone in our home. We didn't know who this person was, what sort of education she had or if IRC even did a background check on her. But we were desperate for help and took a chance. Esmerelda was our in home "teacher" as she called herself. Mid 20's, hispanic, loving girl. Jocelyn lit up when she came over and she was engaged the whole time. Proud, and somewhat embarrassed, I watched Esmerelda interact with my child in ways that I should have been doing, but just didn't know. The first few weeks of her visits and all the neat toys she brought to "hand over hand" play with Jocelyn was an exciting, hopeful time.

One Monday, after she left, I took Jocelyn to the local toy store. I was looking for every toy Esmerelda had and any other developmental toy they had. I was determined to have my 1 year old playing again. *She just needs the right toy that she likes,* I convinced myself. I spent over $800 on toys ranging from squishy "sensory" toys to puzzles, blocks and bubbles. Not the greatest idea when I kept taking time off of work for Jocelyn, but I didn't care. This is my baby and I wwas going to do anything to help her!

Seeing how well Jocelyn was doing with toys and hand over hand play, I thought that maybe she needed to see other kids play. "Modeling" Esmerelda called it. I had friends around the same age as Jocelyn, but the first year of her life, they were painful for me to be around. My baby wasn't doing what their babies were. After Jocelyn turned 1, when things began to change in our home, we had to decline invites to go out to dinner more often than accepting. My quest to find answers filled my calendar and I had no time for anyone. All of our extra income that could've gone to going out, having fun, living life… it all went to sensory toys and gas money to drive to therapy and doctor appointments. It was just an awkward situation now, to have friends. To keep my distance from familiar faces, I decided to enroll Jocelyn in a children's "story time" at our local library.

September 2009: Dennis and I talked about how well Jocelyn did around other kids. I had read different blogs on "delayed" children and how they miraculously weren't "delayed" anymore when the second child came along. "She's doing so much better," I explained to Dennis. "She plays so well with Esmerelda, she loves being around the kids at story time and I think it makes her try harder." Dennis agreed that he saw a positive change in Jocelyn during the past few weeks. We agreed that we should try and have another child.

It was finally something we both agreed on. Something we were both excited for. A glimmer of hope that Jocelyn was going to be just fine AND we were growing our family. Things were looking up! We got pregnant right away in October and we were shocked at how quick it happened. Super excited though. I was really early when I found out, about 5 weeks. At week six, our hope, once again, was ripped away from us when I miscarried. That glimmer of hope, gone over night. The blah atmosphere around the house, with a hint of doubt and questions returned, and made itself right at home as if it had never left.

If I wasn't at a doctor's office on my quest for answers, I was consulting Google or YouTube. It was part of my routine to hop on the computer while Jocelyn took her afternoon nap. One particular summer day, I stumbled across Rett Syndrome. I learned Rett Syndrome usually effects girls. A classic diagnostic sign is "hand wash" (the girls rub their hands as if they were washing them.) Other physical characteristics include small head circumference, small feet, and despite great measures, the inability to gain weight. As I pondered if any of these symptoms fit Jocelyn, I suddenly recalled receiving hand-me-downs from McKenzie just a few months back. Size 7 shoes no longer fit that one year old... Jocelyn wore a size 3! I thought nothing more of it until that moment.

A video about Rett Syndrome showed a clip of a little girl, about 3 years old and she was putting her hands in her mouth- JUST LIKE BABY JO! It was like watching the heartbreaking reflection of my daughter's life.

I lost it.

I felt like I had found something and now that I had found it... I didn't want it anymore! I couldn't breathe. I stood up, I sat down, leaned forward over the counter... trying to find a position where I could catch my breath. The similarities I had found were so obvious. Every time I thought about it, I couldn't breath again. The afternoon suddenly felt hotter. I paced the kitchen with tears and snot all over my face- I found something that fit our issues. It felt like a thousand daggers were just stabbed into my chest! I felt like I was having a panic attack. It was the only way I could breathe. I was happy Dennis at work so he couldn't cast judgement on my episode. I had to get it out. Everything hurt and the world stopped turning.

In the middle of my struggle to remain standing and breathe, I heard sweet noises from the nursery- Jocelyn started to wake. I listened to her joyful babble from her crib, oblivious to the world suddenly stopping. I cleaned up as best I could, picked her up and sat her on my lap in the same oversized recliner we sat in together when I was pregnant with her. I recalled the sleepless night of my baby shower, when I rocked her and rubbed my belly dreamed of what she would look like, what she would be like. When the world was at her feet and the sky was the limit. Dreams of dancing with my daughter, teaching her ballet, doing crafts for the holidays and baking goodies for Daddy. All these things I dreamed when I held her as an infant in that chair, a little more than a year ago, just blew away like dust as I pondered whether Rett Syndrome was what was kidnapping my daughter. My tears started again, I hugged her so tight. Holding onto my daughter while I felt like I lost her at the same time. It made no sense! The world made no sense!

I wanted answers, but did I really?

In the middle of my sobbing-self-pity-party I stopped for a moment and noticed Jocelyn, staring at me. It was the first time I felt like I could really read her face as to what she was thinking: "What's wrong?" Her concerned eyebrows formed by her most adorable pouty lip slowly showing its self. The corners of her mouth bent down. A few short gasps of breath accompanied by two great big crocodile tears from my sweet little girl! The slightest squeal of a cry worked itself out of her. As I watched this unfold, all over again, I fell in love with how adorable she was. Then, like a punch to the gut, I realized, I had made her cry! I worried her! I made her sad and hurt her feelings. I immediately changed my tone and got out my playful voice, smiled real big and consoled her. "HEY, hey, Pretty Girl! It's okay! Nothing's wrong! Mommy is fine, everyone is fine. I love you so much and everything is going to be wonderful, I promise!" At that moment, I vowed that I would never cry in front of her again!

*Elizabeth Jones*

To:
Dr. Geneticist
From:
Elizabeth Jones on behalf of Jocelyn E Jones
Sent:
10/19/2009 8:48 PM PDT
This message is being sent by Elizabeth Jones on behalf of Jocelyn E Jones.


Hello Dr. My name is Beth Jones and you saw my daughter Jocelyn a few months ago. The lab results you ordered are not online so I was hoping you could tell me that we already tested for Rett Syndrome (MECP2) or the atypical Rett (CDKL5) and the tests were negative. If we didn't, can we please order some labs before her follow up in November. Two medical professionals in the past week took a look at Jocelyn and thought Rett's. PLEASE let me know if we already ruled this out. The more research I do on this syndrome, the more my heart aches. Some things seem to fit, but others do not (or that's my denial). This may be a stupid question, but if it is Rett's, we stored stem cells... can we fix it? How can my husband and I be tested for any germlin mutations?

Thank you for your time.
Beth Jones


Dear Mrs. Jones,
We have not tested Jocelyn for Rett syndrome. I understand your concern about this diagnosis. It was not high on my list when I saw her initially, but things can change and evolve, so I'd like to see her on the scheduled appointment on November 2nd. At that time, we'll sit down, go over the consultants' reports, examine her again, and we'll decide what testing is the most appropriate as a next step.

Thanks,
Dr Geneticist

One of Jocelyn's calming mechanisms was going shopping, which I didn't mind. She would be content in the shopping cart while I browsed isles looking at things that I didn't need. I would even turn our shopping distraction time into therapy. With Jocelyn in the bottom of the shopping cart, I would take corners quickly, knocking her slightly off balance, forcing her to use her arms to correct herself or use her trunk muscles to balance. I thought I was a genius.

One particular shopping day she was in the basket and I was reading the back of a book and I heard very VERY loud grunting! "Ohhh no," I laughed to myself. Her little "stork bite" birth mark that had been gone for months now would reappear with every grunt as her face turned beat red. I was in for the mess of a life time and all I could do was laugh as I made my way to the check out. She continued to grunt the entire time, the lady at the check stand got a chuckle out of it too.

I made my way to the Tahoe, I opened the back and turned it into my changing table station. When I undressed Jocelyn, to my great surprise, I found her diaper to be clean! I was so confused, she was pushing this whole time. We wrapped up and started home. On the drive I felt horrible for my daughter! Her little tummy was full and she was trying to work it out. She'd never had an issue with constipation before. *Maybe because she's not walking, like other 15 month olds do,* I thought to myself. Then a thought came to me, *How do other 15 month olds go 'big potty'? They run around, then go squat and hide in a corner, then come out stinky.* Well, maybe I could help Jocelyn with this issue.

As soon as we got home, I put her on a little potty chair I got for my baby shower. I put her in a squat position as she sat on the potty and left her alone. She grunted like she did before. I wasn't sure if I'd find an empty potty like I just found an empty diaper. I gave her a minute and then when the grunting stopped, I helped her up and sure enough, a FULL POTTY! I was ecstatic! Jocelyn giggled with relief and giggled at my screaming and laughing with pride! Dennis was at work, but I had to share the moment with him. I got out my phone, yep, I took a picture and sent it to him with the whole story. He was pretty excited as well. *TAKE THAT!* I thought to myself. For all the doctors, therapists and anyone who ever called Jocelyn "delayed". "Show me a 15 month old that can go big potty on the potty!" I was so proud of her and her accomplishment. A feeling that we should have shared more often at that age, but this was our moment to shine and I couldn't have been happier.

The next day, history repeated itself. The same grunting, position, happy dance, giggles, and yes, even another picture to daddy who was still at work. By the 5th day of this happening, Dennis asked me to please stop sending pictures. I obliged, but the happy dance continued. So did the giggles. Ever since that day, Jocelyn has been "big potty" trained.

Elated that our baby was becoming a toddler, we wanted to feed this growth as much as possible, even with all of her screaming and tantrums some days. Dennis and I assumed Jocelyn might be frustrated that she couldn't walk like the rest of the toddlers, and maybe that was what all the screaming was about. We strived to keep up with our friend's kids and their similar activities. Until we could give Jocelyn a sibling, we decided that "Mommy and Me" classes would suffice. Jocelyn started in December 2009. She lit up like a Christmas tree being around other kids. A hint of hope restored! We had Esmerelda Monday mornings, and Tuesday/Thursday mornings we were at the local town center for our class. Other moms would openly talk to Jocelyn, not blink an eye when I happily answered for her. Some moms were just too uncomfortable to engage, which was fine with me. I was there for Jocelyn, not to make friends. The kids seemed to not even notice she was not walking or talking. It was a great experience, and I carried a little guilt not taking Jocelyn to this sooner.

I tried scheduling all of Jocelyn's appointments on Wednesdays or in the afternoons so she didn't miss any of her lessons, in home or at the town center. When I went back to work, it was mostly weekends and anytime Dennis was off. It was definitely a circus, but we did it. And it was so worth it! We loved seeing her smile and, at times, be indistinguishable amongst the other kids in the class.

# D Day

On a cool January morning in 2010, Grandma Sally accompanied Jo and I for a neurology appointment in Los Angeles. I was in high spirits, ready to show Jocelyn off to the neurologist with how much more alert she was. The neurologist hadn't seen her since the MRI drama. Since our last visit, I had learned how to play with Jo. She was now more motivated and could focus. Sure she couldn't feed herself or pick up toys again yet, but I was confident we would get there. We were on the right path.

I made a presentation book for the neurologist so she could see that Jocelyn had been able to do things. It had a picture (proof) of her doing an activity, and on the opposite page was a 3x5 card with her age at the time the picture was taken, and other notes I might have on the picture. The book went: birth, first year, after her first birthday until her starting to "wake up" the last few weeks. The neurologist, was so sweet. She listened to my every word and made eye contact with me and Jocelyn. She browsed through my presentation with true interest. I absolutely loved her. She explained that the book painted a good picture as to what was going on and she was glad that the Angelman's Syndrome blood test was already ordered and had come back negative. Then she explained that she wanted to test her for Rett Syndrome. My heart sank a little, remembering the YouTube video I had watched a few months prior, but I refused to get upset. *It can't be Rett* I reassured myself. *Jocelyn doesn't hand wring. She is more alert now and getting better, not worse. It's not Rett.*

Then the sweet doctor further explained, "If the test for Rett comes back negative, I will gather resources from other fields and we can all sit in a conference style and see Jocelyn and figure out what is wrong."

I could've kissed her! FINALLY! I had been wanting teamwork this whole time, like an episode of *House,* where something weird is presented and a team gathers and debates on what it could be. Then tests and find answers, and the episode usually always ends with a positive, simple FIX! Oh I was so excited to have a team for Jo. I didn't feel so alone suddenly. I couldn't wait to schedule this pow wow.

"First, we need to get the Rett test and it takes 6-8 weeks for the results," she explained as she handed me the order. This was a special order, not one that could be ordered in the computer. There was paperwork that needed to be filled out, the blood was then shipped to somewhere in Texas. *Probably very expensive,* I thought. Then I read what the doctor wrote under a "reason for test" box: "Patient has no purposeful use of hands". That's the first time I had heard anyone describe Jocelyn like that. I was curious if that was a code for something. I brushed away my question as quickly as it came. *This was going to be a piece of cake,* I thought, *just like the Angelman's test.*

I slowed down on all the other doctor appointments and decided I could put all my eggs in the basket of the neurologist in Los Angeles. I continued with any pending appointments and, of course, Mommy and Me and Esmerelda. But things were coming. Big things! I could feel it! And during this joyful, hopeful time, more excitement: I was pregnant! Dennis and I were excited, again, to grow our family, but decided to wait a while to tell anyone. Especially after what had happened in October!

February 9th we had scheduled a sedative hearing test for Jocelyn as she failed the regular hearing tests a few months prior by not reacting to the noises. "Well, we need to know if she can really hear or not," the Audiologists explained.

"Well she turns and looks at the coffee pot in the morning when it turns on and gurgles. I can tell her 'BOO!' from across the room and she jumps. I think she can hear," I argued.

"That doesn't really mean she can hear," the Audiologist educated.

"Whatever," I complied.

Dennis and I went to this test together, signed the documents, went to a quiet room, once again, allowed someone to drug up our baby... a song and dance that we just wanted to get through. This one was easy, with just a "sleepy" medication- not fully sedated like the MRI. So this was a walk in the park for us parents.

"Where do you want to eat once we bust outta here? Jo's going to be hungry," I whispered to my serious husband.

"Shhhh!" he pointed his index finger to his lips and lectured me to be quiet since Jo was almost asleep. I rolled my eyes and started playing a game on my phone, acting nonchalant, but still watching every move the audiologist, nurse, and Jo made.

About an hour into the whole ordeal, my phone rang. It was not a number I recognized and it was not local. My phone was on vibrate, but in the silent room it seemed loud. Dennis, once again, lectured: "Shhhh!" with his index finger up to his lips. I smushed my phone in attempts for it to not be so loud. "BZZZ" one last time for an alert that a voice mail was left. I would check it later.

"Okay, all done! Everything looks beautiful but the official letter with results will be mailed to you in a few weeks," the audiologist whispered to us. "The nurse just has to recover her and wait for her to wake up before you get to go home."

"Okay, thank you," we both replied. This was Jocelyn's usual nap time so I didn't anticipate her waking for at least another half hour. And that's without being medicated. Now that the test was over, I could check the message:

A nasally voice came on the recorded line, "Hello Mrs. Jones. This is Jane, from the neurologist office in Los Angeles. Doctor wanted me to call you and ask you if you could come in for an appointment tomorrow or on Friday. Please call me directly at…."

I got dizzy, short of breath. We had to be on a waiting list for months and go through a call center to get an appointment with this fabulous doctor. How and why in the world do I get to miraculously come in "tomorrow or Friday" at the drop of a hat?! I tried to reassure myself… *Maybe it's for our episode of House meeting.* Then reason set in. *We weren't going to schedule that until the Rett test came back negative. It's only been 4 weeks since we did the test and she said it'd take 6-8 weeks.* I was about to throw up. I started to sweat. I knew it wasn't the baby, but I lied and blamed it anyway. "Hey babe, I'm feeling a little woosy and I need to go for a walk, okay?" I whispered to Dennis.

"Cool," as he usually answered when I needed to do something.

I gently exited Jocelyn's quiet room and darted to the exit. The hospital was on the same campus as her primary doctor. I got out my cell phone and was shaking too hard to dial the doctor's number. A replay of the MRI drama all over again. I started to pant, heavier now that I didn't have my husband as an audience to upset. *Why is the neurologist calling me?* I finally managed to hit the redial button on my phone for the direct line of the neurologists office.

The nasally voice answered, "Doctor's office?"

"Hi. This is Mrs. Jones. You left me a message about an hour ago about my daughter, Jocelyn?"

"Oh yes, hi Mrs. Jones. So does tomorrow work or would you prefer Friday?"

"I would prefer to know why I am being called for this appointment?" I demanded. I remembered my regret from constantly backing down to the IRC case manager and how it must have delayed things. I was tired of backing down, and this poor lady on the other line was the first to get this side of me.

"Ma'am, I don't know. Doctor just asked me to call you and schedule you in between appointments. Either tomorrow or Friday. Doctor wants to see you," she explained.

"I live two hours away and neither is good for me," I was trying to be difficult and was succeeding. "Please have the doctor call me," I demanded.

"Okay, ma'am. She doesn't really do calls today, but I will ask her."

"Well, she doesn't really have next day appointments available, EVER, either. So I'd like to know what this is about before driving down there!" I sassed back as best as I could, without crying.

I hung up the phone, crossed the parking garage and a little street in the parking lot. I was panting and fighting back tears. A few people glanced over at me concerned. I rolled my eyes in a threatening way, *Don't even THINK about asking me what's wrong.* Strangers kept their distance during my very intentional, emotional walk, which I was grateful for.

Up the elevator, passed the check in desk- I don't even want to deal with those clueless ladies- I need answers! I need Jocelyn's primary doctor. I knew the back way to get passed the locked doors, to the nurses station.

At least something good came of being here the last 6 months; I definitely knew my way around.

Finally, I arrived at Jocelyn's primary doctor's nurse's desk. I was so relieved to be at my destination, as if the answer to why the neurologist was calling was sealed in an envelope sitting on the desk waiting for me. I slumped over on the counter and grabbed onto it for dear life, trying to catch my breath and fighting back tears. I was a hot mess. I wasn't out of shape, it wasn't that I was pregnant, I was just a ball of emotions- a Mama turning into a lioness for the first time. Jocelyn's nurse, who we'd seen so many times over the past few months, looked at me confused. Her co-worker, also confused, looked at me.

"Can I help you?" one of them asked.

I hadn't thought far enough ahead to know what I was going to do once I arrived. "I [pant pant] I need to [pant pant] talk to Jocelyn's doctor," I managed to get out.

"Ohhh, you just missed him- he left campus for meetings the rest of the day," his nurse explained with sincere apologies.

"Well, I need you to look something up," my right hand went straight to my mouth and covered it tightly then my left hand joined it to reinforce the seal. If I spoke what I feared, it would hurt like a thousand swords coming out of my mouth all at once. Tears poured out and gathered in a pool at my right index finger. My nose poured out just as much as my eyes, and it had no where to go. I realized my seal was too tight and I couldn't breathe. I released for a moment, dried my hands on my pants like a 6 year old, not caring if anyone saw or what they thought of me. I was raw... real... and really broken. I had to speak and soon; these nurses were clueless as to how to help me. One started to approach me as if to put her arm around me and console me. I jumped back 3 feet with my arms stretched out to protect myself when I realized what she was about to do. GAURD UP! The nurse froze. I collected myself quickly and very professionally said, "I need you to look in Jocelyn's chart for a blood test result. Her neurologist is trying to get ahold of me and we keep missing each other's call. I need to know those results. This is her primary doctors office, you should have access to that. I know you guys are all computerized, please look up those results!"

"I'm so sorry, Hun. I don't have access to that."

*LIAR!* I thought in my head.

I would lie too if a crazy, panting, crying mom thrashed through my locked ER and demanded test results. I laid my head down on the counter, defeated. Not worth the fight. *This isn't their battle* I told myself, *get it together, Beth, and get out before they call the psych ward!* After a 20 second meditation, I picked my head up, smiled, managed out a whisper, "Thank you ladies, have a nice day," and walked out the door.

My walk back to the hospital side of campus was a long one. The weather was cool and overcast- like my mood. My cell phone started repeatedly ringing. It was Dennis! What was I going to tell him? How could I tell him? I knew something was wrong- the neurologist knew something. The pending test that was supposed to take 6-8 weeks was the only thing she would be calling about. But it's only been 4 weeks... I knew what was wrong, I just had no confirmation. Dennis will want confirmation. He needs to hear it from someone other than me, his neurotic-nurse-wife, whose insisted for the past year that something was wrong with his little girl! I couldn't tell him! What was I going to say?! I was sweating like a pig on a cool February day. I cried off all my makeup. This was going to be hard to hide! He was going to think something was wrong with our baby- OH MY GOODNESS! Our baby- for a minute, I forgot, we are having another baby! Okay, I can't be stressed, I'm pregnant. Some pregnancy book I read said if I have a stressful pregnancy the baby will be a stress case too. I must calm down.

I finally approached Jocelyn's hospital room and walked through the door with a fake smile on my face. Then I looked at Jo, awake, sitting up, smiling and giggling with Daddy, then a real smile came and my heart melted. Dennis demanded "Where were you?" Then he noticed my face and my 'hot mess' look, "What's wrong?!" he panicked.

"I don't want to talk about it right now," I said softly while nodding towards Jocelyn. "Not in front of present company," I explained as I picked her up, snuggled her then put her in her stroller. Dennis accepted my response but was obviously confused and concerned. *I just bought myself a little time to figure out how to tell him,* I thought, while packing up.

We ate some lunch. Then on the car ride home, Jocelyn fell asleep again. We were to expect her to be groggy. While she was sleeping,

I explained to Dennis that the neurologist called and wants to see us tomorrow.

"So," he said, confused as to why I'd be so upset.

"It takes months and a waiting list to get in to see her. The only thing we have going with her right this moment is the Rett test," I explained quickly, hoping if I spoke quickly that it would hurt less, for both of us.

"It's nothing to be upset over, yet," he attempted to reassure me. "You don't know anything for sure yet, I'm sure it's nothing."

Defense and sarcasm was my default. In the silent car, I thought to myself, *Yeah, I'm sure it was nothing that made me pant like a pig, run around the hospital, demanding to talk to doctors and looking like a crazy person. Right…* If he truly believed that it was nothing, I was extremely jealous of his ignorance.

It was 4pm and we were almost home and the neurologist STILL hadn't returned my call! It's been 5 hours. I couldn't take it- I called again, spoke to the same nasally nurse and told her I needed a phone call tonight. I wasn't sure what I would threaten if that didn't happen. I was just trying to be pushy and didn't really know how to be. I could tell the nasally nurse didn't appreciate me and my demeanor so I figured I was accomplishing my "pushy parent" goal, but I didn't care.

We pulled into the garage, unloaded the car, and sat Jocelyn with her toys on the floor which we knew she'd only look at. We put on, "Bee Bo the Sign Language Bear" DVD to kill the silence. I sat at the bar in the kitchen, staring at my cell phone as if that would help it to ring. Dennis stretched and said he was going to go take a nap. I was disgusted at his melancholy and ignored him. Two minutes later, it happened! IT RANG!

I couldn't breathe but, "Hello?" came out of my mouth.

"Mrs. Jones, this is the neurologist in L.A. My nurse said that you requested I give you a call and she said you were pretty demanding about it."

"Yes, I know. I'm sorry. I just have to know why you want to see us tomorrow," I explained.

"Well, Mrs. Jones, I do not like doing this over the phone and I wanted to see you tomorrow to talk about it, but since you are requesting over the phone, I will go ahead. Mrs. Jones, the Rett Syndrome test we were waiting on for Jocelyn came back positive. I am so sorry."

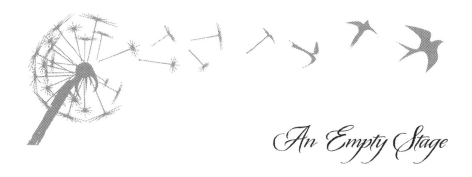

Dennis and I went and spoke with our families individually, without Jocelyn being there. I refused to have anyone crying over her or getting devastating news about defeat- there was, in fact, something wrong with precious Baby Jo. As far as she knew at 21 months old, everything was the same as it was yesterday. When we went to our parents and my grandparents, we were each short and sweet "She has Rett Syndrome," and then bailed out of there. We did not want anyone crying on my shoulder. I didn't want to see anyone cry about our "situation". Abort! Abort! as soon as the words fell out of my mouth. Home- to hold Jo and to process.

Next step: tell the world. I didn't want to call anyone. I didn't want to answer questions. I had enough questions of my own. Facebook! I would use Facebook! I had never posted anything before. I thought it was silly and I didn't understand it. Months prior, I made a profile and found some old friends, but didn't do much past that. So sitting in my sorrow, I finally found a useful purpose for social media:

"Hello family and friends. We received news Tuesday of a diagnosis for Jocelyn's delay: Atypical Rett Syndrome. Learn about it at www. rettsyndrome.org. Prayers are welcomed. Our first fundraiser is Saturday, see www.firstgiving.com/babyjo That's all for now."

We got many LIKES, condolences and, "Let me know what I can do…" The fundraiser, I directed everyone to, was a stroll-a-thon, which I randomly found on a Google search, the night of the diagnosis. "Southern California Rett Picnic" which to me was such an oxymoron! Nothing about Rett is a picnic! But I had questions and if there were families there

that could answer questions, I had to go! But I was embarrassed to go empty handed. Hence, the Facebook post for helpless feeling friends to donate, if they wanted to. With that simple post, we raised $2,100 in 3 days. I was grateful, yet shocked! I didn't realize how much people cared or wanted to help. My first humbling experience which I didn't know how to handle…

The picnic was horrible; for me at least. We had a whole team of Dennis' immediate family, my mom, Aunt Lori, and Crystal Gax ("Gax")- one of my bridesmaids. Sally made shirts for our team and ironed on a picture of Jocelyn. They were cute, but I hated it! I hated everything about what I was forcing myself to do. To make things worse, all the Rett families were so welcoming, happy to meet us, eager to help "the newly diagnosed baby, the youngest we've seen diagnosed…" I watched the other Rett girls all over the place. Some walking, some in giant wheelchairs, some "hand washing" while others hand-mouthed so bad they were choking on their knuckles!

I became nauseous! Possibly because I was pregnant, but no one there knew that, except Dennis and Gax. But it was more than just annoying pregnancy nausea. It was the horrible realization that I was starring at my future. I fought for months and months to get answers. Now that I had them, I didn't want them at all. I thought that if I had answers to Jocelyn's delay then I could fix it. Looking at all the older girls, and listening to their parents attempt to give me reassurances that I was living the "hard time of Rett right now" and "it gets easier." I understood that I was walking through all the stages of grief:

- ⋆ Denial- Dennis and I both wanted to repeat the blood test for the diagnosis. In some moments, we just didn't think it fit Jocelyn. Especially after seeing other girls with Rett.
- ⋆ Anger- Oh the anger! I hated everyone, truly, I did. I hated Crystal and Kristin and their healthy kids McKenzie and Jacob. Full of hate and envy! I was becoming a very ugly person!
- ⋆ Bargaining- I raised a lot of money in 3 days for Rett Syndrome- I figured perhaps there would be a reward that Jocelyn wouldn't get all the horrible side effects I learned about: seizures, scoliosis, the need for a feeding tube…

* Depression- yes, that was obvious. I tried so hard to not be depressed, for Jocelyn, but also for the baby I was carrying. In the dozens of pregnancy books and articles I read, they all claimed that being stressed during pregnancy results in a stressed out baby! I didn't want to fail my second child, like I felt like I had failed Jocelyn.

* Acceptance- here's where I had a problem. The attempted reassurance that, "It get's easier," by other Rett parents, felt like, with time, I would accept this defeat against my daughter. I never, NEVER wanted to reach acceptance! (And I still haven't to this day!)

After the fundraiser, Dennis and I went home and locked the door. For weeks! We had enough! We didn't want the sympathetic, "I'm so sorry" look from anyone. We did our part- we fundraised a bit. Now we just wanted to be alone! Even from our families. I still hated everyone, I'm sure they could tell. I just wanted to be alone! And thats exactly how I felt. ALONE!

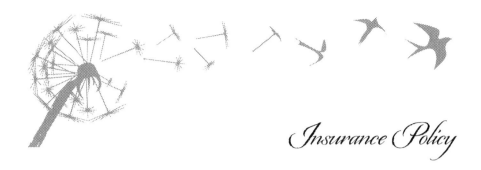

I laid in the gurney watching every heart beat of the fetal monitor. Dennis and I were excited, feeling like experts since we had been down this road before. This time it would be less chaos. We were 4 weeks early, but Rylee Erin Jones announced she was ready to meet the world when my water broke that morning. I was worried about contractions, but didn't feel anything yet.

"We could still do a V-Bac," I questioned Dennis from across the room.

"NO! No surprises. It's too dangerous and we already have enough on our hands," Dennis firmly kiboshed.

I laid back down disappointed but agreed . I've been told it is dangerous to have a vaginal delivery after a c-section. Dangerous for both baby and mom. I wanted to do it so bad, just to experience true birth, but I couldn't be selfish. "The point is to have a baby, no matter how it comes," I remember my mom telling me a few weeks prior. So I laid there and waited.

The nurse came in, "The OR is almost ready, but the doctor ordered some nausea medicine before delivery. Medication XXX." I looked at Dennis and he realized it was the same medication Jocelyn had when she was 4 months old. The nurse gave it in my IV, then as she she walked out, she informed, "I'll be back in a bit."

Moments later I felt my heart racing. I had to get up. "Dennis, I have to go to the bathroom," I lied. He helped unhook the monitor and held my hand as I walked to the bathroom within my hospital room. I stood there and looked in the mirror. I didn't even try to go to the bathroom,

I just felt like I had to walk. My breathing got faster. It felt like a panic attack. *What in the world is going on?* I thought. *Something's wrong, I don't want to do this!* I walked out of the bathroom and started walking about the hospital room collecting our things.

"Let's go" I instructed Dennis as he peered from his cell phone game.

"It's not time yet, Beth. Sit down," he answered confused.

"No, I mean home. I don't want to do this. Let's go, I'm done," I argued.

"Get your butt back on the gurney and wait," he threatened. I complied with a sigh and a squat. Then up again and moving about the room. Dennis, irritated, watched as I was being defiant to his request.

The nurse, very bubbly, came back, "Okay, lets go have a baby! Honey, get back in bed," she asked politely.

"No, I'd like to go home now," I argued.

"Umm, no. You can't go home. Your water broke, you have to have your baby today. Please get in bed!" I glanced at Dennis and saw the look of relief on his face that he had someone on his side.

I didn't want to be an annoying patient so I listened to the nurse but still protested, "I'm okay," I panted. "I don't feel right. Something's not right!" The nurse left the room. My ER nurse thoughts started racing and I started wondering if this was "impending doom". I've seen it several times. A sick patient suddenly becomes very anxious, uncooperative, then suddenly "codes", "flatlines", dies right before your eyes.

The nurse barged in through the door with the doctor. The doctor calmly explained, "Elizabeth, I think you are having a reaction to Medication XXX. This happens sometimes with this medication. I'm going to give you an antidote- this will calm you down. We are wheeling you into the OR now to have a baby. Congratulations."

My thoughts were spinning. I've given "Medication XXX" so many times in the ER for nausea. I knew the side effects, but actually experiencing it was another thing. I wanted to crawl out of my skin. I wanted to pace the room, walk out of the hospital, go home- WHILE IN ACTIVE LABOR!

As the antidote filled my veins, I started to feel overcome with peace and relief. Being wheeled down the hallway, all I could think of was Jo. My experience just then, with "Medication XXX" was so horrible and it was only 20 minutes. I gave that medication to her for 3 days- at the young age of 4 months! I felt like a horrible mother. Would she ever forgive me? Why did I do that to her?

Thirty minutes later, we were in a familiar setting: blue drapes, me tied up unable to move and Dennis in his yellow jump suit. "You look hot Babe! I love the cap! You would've made a sexy surgeon." I passed the time with conversation.

Embarrassed from the compliment Dennis ignored it and changed the subject,   "The doctor is literally throwing elbows to get Rylee out. Wow! Do you feel that?!"

"Thanks Babe, shut up please! You're lucky my hands are tied down or I'd beat you," I jokingly threatened.

"You'd have to catch me first and you can't feel your legs," he joked back.

"Here she is, it's a girl!" the doctor proudly announced.

I smiled, teared. Dennis stayed at my side. We waited, and waited. The most horrible loudness of silence.

"Why isn't she crying?" I asked calmly. Dennis' face was a little green. I could read concern. No one answered me. "Why isn't she crying?!" I demanded louder, helplessly tied to the bed, paralyzed. Dennis wasn't invited over to see her yet as he was with Jocelyn.

"Hey guys, how's it going over there?" the doctor called to the other side of the room to the nurses.

"DENNIS?!" my eyes filled with worried tears.

"Calm down, it's okay," he calmly reassured me, regardless of the fact that he was just as clueless as I was. He probably had the same calm demeanor at work if he found a screaming victim in a burning building. "It's okay..." oh it made me sick with envy.

"WAAAAA!" we heard her first high pitched cry. The whole room sighed with relief. I cried.

"Is her cry high pitched?" I asked towards the ceiling, intending for anyone to answer. I remember in nursing school that high pitched screams were a sign that something was wrong.

Again, I was ignored.

The nurse walked by with Rylee all bundled up, her head sticking out, not crying. She was so tiny, adorable, and looked nothing like

Jocelyn, which for some reason, I expected her to. I smiled and waved my restrained hand. Dennis got to hold her first and sat next to my head with her for a minute. She was very quiet, but so beautiful. Dennis held his trophy proud. I was so in love, with both of them.

"Okay," the nurse interrupted after a minute or two. "We will meet you in recovery after you are stitched up."

"Dennis, follow them!" Again, a familiar first experience of separation anxiety. This time with my second bundle of joy.

Finally arriving to the recovery room, there they were. I got to hold her "chest to chest, skin to skin" which was encouraged for bonding and for nursing. As this tiny puppy sized baby laid on me, I enjoyed every cuddle, but my ER nurse brain fired up again. "Is she grunting," I softly asked and was ignored. I knew grunting was a sign of struggling to breath. I looked over at her oxygen level on the monitor. It read 88%.

*NO!* I yelled at God in my head. *No way! I saw all throughout my pregnancy signs at Hobby Lobby, posts on Facebook 'God will only give you what you can handle'. GOD!* I threatened in my head *I cannot handle this! She is to be my healthy, easy baby! I've had my difficult child. FIX THIS NOW!* I threatened. Then a hint of guilt set in my head as I thought, *Had I delivered vaginally, it would have forced secretions out of her lungs and she could be breathing better right now? Why did I do that? I'm always making the wrong decision for my children!*

The recovery nurse interrupted my fit in my head by pounding on Rylee's back, "Come on little girl. You need to do a little bit better." She seemed worried. I glared at her in search of answers. She felt my concern and explained, "She isn't breathing as good as she should be. She might need to go to the Neonatal Intensive Care Unit. I'm waiting for the neonatologist to come."

I sat in silence with complete confidence that she wouldn't need to go to the NICU. *Nope!* I convinced myself. *This is promised to be my easy child. I can't handle any more drama. She just needs skin to skin. She needs her Mommy. God wont do this to me. She will be my healthy child. I can't handle any more drama and God knows that.* Two minutes later, the neonatologist walked in, took one look at Rylee and said, "Hi Mrs. Jones. Your baby needs to come with me to the NICU."

I laid in recovery, alone. Very alone. I didn't even have my baby bump belly to rub anymore. I sat and became angry. Mad with my circumstances! Mad... with God!

My rapid thoughts lead me to when I was 16 years old, safe, no cares in the world other than the dramas of high school and my job at the local drug store. I worked hard, was never late, got good grades, paid for everything myself- even my new to me car. Things were great. Easy...

I reflected on one night in particular. I liked having the TV on in my room while I would fall asleep. Infomercials were the best. So I had it on my usual 9pm "infomercial" channel. This particular night, they weren't selling a slicer and dicer or work out video. There were bald kids, soft music, and movie stars asking for help! Intrigued, I turned the volume up. The broadcast was for St. Jude's Children's Hospital- raising money for children's cancer treatments and research to cure them. My heart bled with sadness. *They're just kids! This is the saddest thing ever!* I called my mom in the room to watch, thinking I was going to show her something she didn't know yet.

"Yeah, Beth. Kids get cancer. Sometimes they die. I see it all the time" she calmly stated. That was a pivotal moment where I gained a better understanding of what my mom did at work. She was a pediatric nurse, certified in oncology. CLICK, I got it! Light bulb on!

"WE NEED TO DO SOMETHING! Call that 800 number and donate, Mom!" tears pouring down my face.

"I do donate, Beth. You donate," she suggested then calmly left my room. Still shocked about these kids suffering and the sudden realization of what my mom did at this job of hers, I was baffled. I made chump change, how could I give anything that mattered or made a difference?

Then, Jennifer Aniston came on the TV and answered my questions "Anything will help. If you can give ANYTHING, please call now". Okay, they could use my help too. I suddenly remembered a credit card Aunt Lori Dechant got me to use to build my credit. I found it, called, and donated $25. As I hung up, I felt a peace come over me. I helped! But not only did I help, I probably wont ever have a sick child! I supported, I helped... I'm in the clear!

My thoughts returned to the recovery room as a nurse started to wheel me to the medical floor.

"NO! I want to see my baby! We need to do chest to chest bonding!" I was so envious that Dennis got to be with her and I couldn't. I knew I was freshly sliced from hip to hip, even though I couldn't feel anything. I knew if I tried to get out of bed, things could go bad quick.

I quickly changed my tone with the nurse, knowing I wouldn't get what I wanted if I was a brat: "Please, can we stop by the NICU so I can see her again?"

"I'm not supposed to, but okay." Down the hall in my gurney we went. Finally after major security doors, we wheeled into a large room with tiny incubators everywhere. As a nurse, I could recognize some of the problems with the babies. I was upset that my new baby was labeled as "critical", just as these, obviously worse off babies, were. I finally got to her bed and her eyes were open, still not crying, just checking things out. I reflected on when Jocelyn was tiny, an hour new, checking out the world. But she was in my arms! Rylee was in a bed, hooked up to an IV and oxygen. I tried not to cry in front of her- like I do Jocelyn. I didn't want Rylee to feel my anxiety. Her nurse came over and was very compassionate:

"Hi Mom! She's doing good. Hopefully she'll just need a few hours of this. She even had her first dirty diaper."

WHAT?! I freaking missed it?! That was one of the highlights of Jocelyn's births- Dennis changing her never ending "potty". Something we sill laughed about. Done- gone! I missed it! She was an hour old and I already missed a moment of her life! I was infuriated!

"Please let me know when I can come feed her. I really want to breastfeed my baby!" I begged her nurse.

"Okay, it'll be a while until you can get out of bed, but when you can, come down and we will make that happen, no problem" she reassured me.

Up to my room I went. I had to go on a different floor than postpartum because I was "a mommy without a baby". It made sense to me as a nurse, to separate the mommies with babies from the other hormonal moms who maybe lost their baby during delivery, or with really bad off babies who and had to go to the NICU. But as the patient, as the mom, I was heartbroken! Wheeling me farther and farther away from my newborn, different level floors even.

Alone in my room again, I was beating myself up! I felt I was failing, again and again.

* I should've done the V-bac! Then all Rylee's secretions in her lungs would've been forced out during delivery and she could be breathing on her own.
* I should've refused Medication XXX
* I failed at nursing Jocelyn and not being with Rylee the first hours of her life are setting me up for failure to nurse her!
* Is Rylee going to be okay? Is she going to have oxygen deprived brain injury? Every new doctor we ever visited with Jocelyn focused primarily on the delivery and pregnancy. Now I've failed at that, TWICE.
* Is Rylee going to be labeled as FAILURE to thrive now too?
* Failed
* Failure
* FAILURE!
* "Mommy without her baby" floor
* A Rett mom
* Special needs mom! and will it be of TWO now, because of my failure!

A fit began internally in my lonely room. *All these labels, categories, "clubs" I am in and want out! I hate it! This isn't how it's supposed to be! We waited to have kids until we were married. We waited to get married until we had a house and were in our careers. I requested, at the alter, healthy children! Not this! "A touch of asthma" is all I said I could handle. My first, and now my second! Are you freaking kidding me God? Are you not listening to me? I'm a good person! Dennis is a good person! We did everything right! I even donated to St. Jude's Children's Hospital when I was 16! I had invested in the promise for healthy children my whole life! What kind of sick God are you?!*

Tears in my eyes, soreness in my incision and not able to feel my feet even a little, I called for my nurse. I told her I needed to go nurse my baby. She rounded up a nursing assistant and a wheel chair and they took me down. I didn't care about me. The first hours are the most important, for bonding, for nursing. I had this crazy imagination that Rylee would be bonding with an IV pump and not me! Determined, angry, and numb, down I went to the NICU to feed her every one and a half hours!

During an evening feed, I called for my wheelchair taxi and it was taking forever! The NICU nurse called my room and asked me to hurry because Rylee was really hungry. I didn't wait. With numb legs I left my room, walked down the stairs, and fed her. *How's that for a fight, God?! I will not let this stop me! Look, I'm a fighter. Now please, give me a reward in this mess and get us out of here safely and without harm!*

Sitting and feeding Rylee was amazing. She did so good, she was a pro! Such a trooper! So calm, no crying, just got down to business and ate until she was full. Then she'd look around so curiously. As I held her, I started to doze in the chair- immediately, the nurse came and told me I had to go to my room and get rest. It was horrible leaving her, but I could've slept anywhere at that point, I obliged.

# Jocelyn's Journey's Birth

Within a few weeks, we were finally in a bit of a routine as a family of 4. Rylee's was showing no signs of problems from her one night stay in the NICU at birth. She was nursing great and was pretty content. At 4 weeks, Dennis went back to work and I was alone with two kids. Jocelyn had over 24 hours a week of in-home applied behavioral analysis (ABA) therapy, which helped so much with the transition of a new baby being in the house. Jocelyn had one on one attention Monday through Friday during the day, with a therapist so I could give attention to Rylee. When the therapists would leave, Rylee would swing in the baby swing and then I would get Jo all to myself.

I had the days figured out. It was the nights I struggled with. During this time, a side of Rett reared it's ugly face on my sweet Jocelyn… "sleep disturbances". Rylee would be up the first half of the night nursing. Then, when Rylee finally would be sound asleep at 1 a.m., Jocelyn would wake up at 2 a.m. laughing. Non-stop laughing. For hours. Two weeks into this, I started to think it was a seizure. This went on for months. I dreaded the night time! I never slept. I became mean and couldn't stand her 2 a.m. laugh! *What kind of mother can't stand the sound of her child's laugh?!* Apparently, this one! Not only could I not stand it because I couldn't sleep, but I couldn't stand it because it wasn't normal- it wasn't Jocelyn laughing. It was some random electrical or chemical abnormality in her brain, firing away and making her laugh uncontrollably. It infuriated me, knowing this Rett Beast had control over my daughter, all hours of the day and night!

The days following those sleepless nights were difficult. While Jocelyn was in the other room having therapy, I would hold Rylee in front of the computer. I was, once again, researching on what to do for Jocelyn. Sleep was the research topic at this time. I was turning into a sleep deprived crazy person! My internet digging seemed to always lead me to scientific Rett research, specifically, Rett Syndrome Research Trust (RSRT).

I was instantly intrigued with RSRT and their optimism of curing Rett Syndrome in the near future. They website laid out a timeline for Rett Syndrome- the gene was discovered in 1999 by Dr. Zoghbi. Up until that point, Rett Syndrome was diagnosed only by symptoms. In 2007, Dr. Bird genetically engineered a mouse with Rett Syndrome and then REVERSED it! When he reversed the Rett Syndrome, the mouse was at the end of it's life span- it was an adult. This proved that Rett Syndrome wasn't a degenerative disorder. I absolutely loved watching the video of the mouse with Rett Sydrome, not walking, hand washing, rocking back and forth. THEN, after "putting back the missing gene" as Dr. Bird described, the mouse was perfectly normal! Walking, feeding itself, no longer hand wringing. A beautiful two minute video to watch in the middle of hatred for Rett! I would watch the video over and over and over. I would cry and dream of Jocelyn, like the mouse, suddenly gaining all the skills she had lost over the last year and a half. I noticed that both of these doctors, who pioneered the way for curing Rett Syndrome, were on the RSRT Scientific Advisory Board. RSRT was also funding current Rett Syndrome research projects by these doctors. The best of the best were with RSRT and making huge progress in (scientifically) a short amount of time! It gave me something I hadn't had in over a year, HOPE!

With all I was learning about RSRT, my internet search went from looking for "how to get Jocelyn to sleep", to "how can Jocelyn be cured!" Getting her to sleep at night was just a bandaid to treat one of the many challenges she was currently facing. Since diagnosis, Dennis and I had learned so much about what Jocelyn's future potentially held: feeding tubes, seizures, anxiety, self inflicted injuries, scoliosis, cardiac problems… just to name a few. I didn't want to spend my time worrying how I would put "bandaids" on all of these potential future issues. I wanted to put my time and energy into preventing them from happening: to CURE Jocelyn!

My mom and I talked about the foundation frequently, and one day, we finally decided to call the number on the bottom of the website. To our surprise, Monica Coenraads, Executive Director and Co-founder answered the phone! Monica was sweet, extremely down to earth and asked us so many questions about Jocelyn and our family. Monica also shared with us about her family, including her 14 year old daughter, Chelsea, who had Rett Syndrome. I was in aw of her, having a Rett girl and finding a way to be so involved with Rett research and creating RSRT. She was incredible! Monica asked us if we'd be interested in helping her by fundraising to support RSRT research projects. Honestly, my mom and I were a bit bashful, having never done anything like this before. We told Monica we would think about it. She was extremely supportive and understanding. Monica explained a little of what her most successful events entailed and how to get started, just so that we knew what we'd be getting into if we decided to help. She was sincerely caring and personable. An all around likable person, and what an amazing woman to be able to care for her daughter and run RSRT! I was impressed and felt a little out of my league.

The next few nights after meeting Monica on the phone were sleepless nights. Not because of our conversation, but because of Rett Syndrome consuming my daughter with uncontrollable laughter. I felt like a horrible mother for being so exhaustedly irritated with the sound of my own child's laugh. That's when I had enough. I was ready to fight back- fight this Rett Beast! The only way to beat it was to cure it! I called Monica and told her we were in! She was elated and extremely grateful to have our help. Monica gave us direction on where to begin and what to do to start having an "event" for RSRT.

I was excited to help, to fight back, to have somewhere effective to put whatever energy I had into. However, I felt I was biting off a bit more than I could chew. Thankfully, my mom took the reins and, with mine and Dennis' permission, she began figuring out what we had to do. She gathered a timeline and a list of things we needed: a name for the event, a committee, a venue, food, tickets, invitations, and people! I was hopeful, I was excited, but I was exhausted and still grieving. When Dennis and I gave her permission to do the gala, it was with the intentions of just doing one event. We can help contribute to Jocelyn's cure, but we were safe in isolation and strived and longed to be a "normal" family! Asking our friends and family to pay to come hang out with us at a party didn't seem normal to us at all.

I remember my mom giving many suggestions for a name. "Jocelyn's Dream" "Cure Jocelyn"... most I don't remember. But then one day, I remember driving down Dale Evan's Parkway and suddenly, it popped into my head "Jocelyn's Journey". It wasn't just a dinner we would be sharing, it was everything that we had been through over the last 3 years. The journey to get her diagnosed. The silent struggle, no one knew about. It had been a journey and I was ready to share! I called my mom to tell her the name of our gala, and she loved it. We were a go!

At this point, it felt so good to have something to work towards. On bad Rett days, I worked on the event planning- refusing to be defeated by the Rett Beast! I had a long time friend, Marjorie, who ran the catering department at Granite Hills High School. When I explained our event to her, she was delighted to help! It was so hard to ask for help, from anyone! Dennis and I are a "do it yourself" kind of people and we didn't like handouts. Prideful, looking back now! So when someone was delighted to help donate 200+ meals?! It was very humbling for us!

Uncle Bary graciously signed up to be our audio/visual and technical support. RSRT said they'd design and give us the invitations. There was another Rett organization, "Rocky Mountain Rett Association," who received more gifts than they needed, from the department store Sears. They donated many wonderful gifts to Jocelyn's Journey including a big screen TV, video games and players, Macbook, a vacuum... many impressive things. So our auction/raffle was pretty much settled... It seemed too easy, too good to be true.

We were well on our way and Monica was readily available at the drop of a hat, anytime we had a question or a problem. When word spread on what we were doing, the outpour of positive responses was mind-blowing. Everything was coming together nicely; however, I began to dread the night of the event as it grew closer. I thought I was excited and ready to share with the world, but realized I was more comfortable in isolation. I was still secretly full of hate and envy for other "typical" families. It was so nice to feel supported, but at the same time, Dennis and I both wished we were never in the situation to begin with. That our daughter wasn't suffering. That we didn't need the help... but we did. We knew, soon, we'd have to face the crowd of supporters and share with them, Jocelyn's Journey.

*Back Porch Confessions*

In the midst of all the planning of an event, the 24 hours a week of strangers in our home for therapy, and adjusting to a new born consumed me. Dennis was, regrettably, on my back burner with how he was dealing with everything. He was quiet, as usual, and let me do whatever I wanted. He generally stayed out of my way and helped out when I needed something. Staying busy was a coping mechanism of mine. Dennis, was just… quiet. For a long time.

A few months before our event, Dennis went to a bachelor party at the river. I was happy for him to get away and let loose a little. No responsibilities and maybe he'd get some sleep. Sleep just wasn't happening at that time in our home. I was happy for the bachelor and happy to see a bunch of knuckle head boys get together and celebrate, like the good 'ol days.

When the weekend was over and he was getting dropped off at home, I got a pat on the back from Ryan, Dennis' best man at our wedding. He leaned in and whispered to me, "You need to talk to your husband, he had an episode." Confused and concerned I returned to the house and made dinner. Dennis napped on the couch, exhausted from a weekend of too much fun, I assumed. *Episode? Dennis would occasionally sleep walk, but why do I need to talk to him about that…?*

7 p.m. rolled around and it was time for my usual "lay in bed and struggle to get sleep while my two girls took turns being awake all night". But this hot summer night, Dennis went on the back porch, so I decided I'd sleep next year and went to join him. I asked how his weekend was.

He shared a few funny stories- boys being boys. Then he opened up for, perhaps, the first time in our entire marriage.

"I kinda lost it one night," he confessed quietly.

"What happened?" I softly encouraged him to continue.

"I don't know. We were outside and we started talking about Jocelyn and I just had a fit."

"Okay, well, honestly Dennis, I'm glad. You can't keep that in."

"There's more."

Silence. For minutes. I waited patiently for my husband to collect himself and be able to speak. I sat and admired our view of the mountains afar. Our beautiful green grass that needed to be mowed. I looked over to the area of grass Dennis was trenching for sprinklers, years ago, when I told him we were having our first child. It felt like yesterday, yet at the same time, a life time ago.

"How could God let this happen? She's so perfect and everything was going so good. I really don't think there is a God if something like this could happen." For the first time since the day Jocelyn was diagnosed, my husband shed some tears. That killed me more than anything. Never do I want to see my husband hurt!

"Okay," I replied calmly.

"You're okay with that? That I don't believe in God?"

"Welp, Dennis," I had no clue how these words so confidently fell out of my mouth, they just did. "Do you believe in Hell? That there is evil in the world?"

"Yes," he whispered confidently.

"Well, I don't think you can believe in one and not the other. I think you are mad at God, and that's okay, so am I. And I think that's normal. To the point where you want to reject him. I understand. And you know what, He's God. He can handle it!" I was shocked at how much sense I made.

"I was so scared to tell you that I don't believe in God, I thought you would want a divorce" he explained with relief.

"Dennis, first of all, I don't believe that to be true. That you don't believe in Him. I believe you are mad at Him. Secondly, I wouldn't divorce you over that. I know you will come around. Time will reveal things. Yes, this sucks! Yes, I hate so many things including the tired zombie, grouch I am. But it wont be like this forever. Give yourself time."

We sat in comfortable silence and I started to doze off. Dennis nudged me and told me to go to bed. Gratefully, I obeyed. We didn't speak of this again, nor did I see Dennis shed tears over Jocelyn again- until the night of the Jocelyn's Journey Gala.

September 24, 2011 came so quickly. Our big event was finally here. A year of work and planning and it was show time. Tables were decorated with plastic yellow table cloths- Jocelyn's favorite color. Small center pieces on each table, a jazz trio for live music sat in one corner of the room and opposite them were fold up tables with ice chests to make the bar. The committee was running around, doing last minute set up tasks. Everyone was dressed in cocktail dresses and casual collars. It was fun to see everyone so dressed up- like at a wedding! I usually loved getting all dressed up and having a party to go to, however, this was different. I wasn't looking forward to this party like I would a Christmas party or a wedding. All eyes were on me and my family, and I wanted to disappear!

When the doors opened, I sat in the front of the room holding Jo. I admit, I was hiding. This was the night I asked everyone to come to, and pay to be a part of, and all I could do was sit and hold Jo and pray no one would come talk to us. I didn't want anyone to see Jocelyn throw a fit, because it was her "difficult" time of day. I didn't want to give a fake smile to all of our guests. I fought tears every second I sat in that chair, and I blamed Jocelyn being tired for my antisocialness. I feared that if I got up I would get apologetic smiles from people I hadn't seen in a while. I feared to be pitied. For Jocelyn to be pitied. It was the most powerful mix of emotions: gratitude for people coming to our event, but prideful, wanting to put on a "nothing's wrong with us" attitude. Worst of all, I feared that someone would sense my pride, and desire to be left alone and interpret it as me not being grateful. I was paralyzed with emotions and the safest place I found was sitting at the table, alone, protecting my little cub.

I then realized the irony of our theme being the color yellow (Jocelyn's favorite color at the time). I was acting it out… a yellow coward! I hated Rett more than ever as I held Jo in my lap even tighter. I never dreamed I would be hosting an event to save my daughter's life. That is exactly how I saw it, and still do today. Luckily, Dennis and Rylee worked the room and greeted everyone cheerfully and chatted away. I envied their energy and ability to be social. I didn't trust myself to try.

Dinner was prepared and catered by Granite Hills High School students, and it was amazing! I loved having high school kids involved with our event. I was too selfish in high school to be involved with a charity. I was so proud of each kid and I was more comfortable talking to all of them, that evening, than anyone else. All of our guests were very impressed with the food and the service. After dinner, I finally started to loosen up, until it was time for the "entertainment" of the evening. It started with a homemade video I put together about Jocelyn's journey. From her regression to diagnosis. The first five seconds the movie started to play, my social butterfly husband turned into a sobbing mess. I pulled on his arm and pleaded, "What is wrong with you?! You've seen this movie 1000 times! Stop it, we have to speak right after this!" The flood gates opened on me then too. You could hear a pin drop in the room, and I am uncertain how many people heard my plead to Dennis to stop crying.

When the ten minute movie finally ended, we were up. We had written a speech the week prior and decided that we would take turns on topics. I allowed us a break in the middle of our speech with an intermission video. It was two minutes of Jocelyn's progress during therapy. My precious moments of her successes over the year, which I happened to capture on video. I wanted to show our guests what Jocelyn could do! During the intermission video, we took sips of water, collected ourselves, held onto each other, then resumed with our turns speaking. When Dennis spoke, he would cry and the entire room would be sobbing. It was kind of like a wedding. No one cares when the bride cries, that's to be expected. But when the groom cries, LOOK OUT! And I have to admit, him crying made it hard for me to stand and keep going as well. I couldn't bare to see my private, calm, cool, collective, husband crying in front of a room of 200 people. I was so proud of him though, pulling through, getting it done and all because he loved his daughter so much and would do anything for her!

I wanted to make what we went through during Jocelyn's regression, relatable to the guests. It wasn't likely any of them knew of Rett Syndrome before that evening, so it was their first exposure. But, more than likely, most of them have seen a stroke victim before. So I used the analogy of having a patient in the ER experiencing stroke symptoms. Being able to speak yesterday, but today cannot. Could use their hands yesterday, but now cannot. Some have seizures, some have feeding tubes. Some are worse off than others. How frustrating for stroke victims to lose what they used to have. And how frustrating for Rett girls, at the young age of 1-2 years, to have lived the same traumatic experience.

We did it! We were done! Dennis and I were both a mess and as we took our seats, everyone clapped and Dennis and I had a very long hug. We were more holding each other up from the emotional accomplishment we just experienced. TOGETHER! We did it together! The hardest part of the entire year, was done! We were breathing better and even holding hands under the table. It definitely brought us closer together than we had been all year.

After the raffle, auction, bar, and other donations, the evening raised $53,000 for RSRT! Myself, Dennis, the committee... everyone was very pleased! Routine fundraiser attendees in our community were shocked at how much we raised. It felt good to do our part to help research along. Post event, people continued to reach out to us and offered to help with "next year". I would answer with a chuckle, "No... this was a one time thing. There wont be a 'next year'. Thank you though."

# Shaking Things Up a Bit

Come February 2012, I got an uneasy feeling in my gut about Jocelyn and her cure. Guilt, perhaps for not supporting RSRT like we did last year. It took a few days, but I finally went to Dennis.

"I think I want to have another event."

"Are you out of your mind?! We have people in our house 24/7 already with therapy. We are nowhere near being the 'normal' family that we always try to be. We can't even have time for ourselves. We did our part, Beth. Let someone else have an event!"

"I can't just sit here, Dennis, and let this happen to her."

It took a few days for him to come around. I told him the date of the first committee meeting and he looked at me as he rolled his eyes and sighed, "Whatever, Elizabeth!"

This year I was determined to be more focused, more grateful for our guests and not just hide in the corner during the event. *I can do better than what I did last year* I scorned myself. Suddenly, I wasn't afraid anymore to ask for help. I knew that this year was going to be more work: we didn't have the gifts from Rocky Mountain Rett Association that we had last year, we now had to get our own invitations... I mailed a flyer to our friends and family members asking if they'd be interested in helping us with the 2012 event and join the Jocelyn's Journey Committee. Fifteen people ended up coming to our house for the first meeting and joined the committee. I was humbled, already, just on the support we had to help with the event! I shared with the committee, on the first meeting, that it was going to be a bit stressful, especially toward the end. "It's like planning a wedding, on a $0 budget. So you have to get everything we need donated... LET'S GO!"

Our event was very lean with so little overhead. We learned this from Monica, herself. RSRT prides itself on 96% of every donated dollar goes directly to research. Little overhead! I didn't realize how some non-profits have extremely high overhead (the leaders of some non-profits pay themselves way too much money!) I didn't even realize that there were non-profits that were so shady; asking for money but not using it for the cause they were "supporting". The integrity of RSRT being so lean made me love Monica even more! The Jocelyn's Journey event took her lead on this and every sponsor, ticket sale and any funds brought in the night of the gala would go to RSRT, not to throwing the event. We did have some overhead, but we decided to do "side fundraisers" such as selling Jocelyn's Journey bracelets for $5 to cover costs.

I was determined to do things a little different all around for year two. Striving to be better. Social media can be a blessing for a Rett parent; learning from other Rett parents, getting tips, hearing other experiences... However, it can also be heart wrenching. That March, in one of my Rett Syndrome support groups on Facebook, I learned about an 11 year old girl, Arianna, loosing her battle to Rett Syndrome. "Sudden, unexplained death," is a complication of Rett. Arianna was my first. I held Jocelyn a little tighter that night. Then I went back to work on our Jocelyn's Journey gala, in honor of Arianna. I became honest and loud on my personal Facebook site. I shared what little I knew of Arianna's story and I begged for anyone to help. Sponsors, donations, ticket sales or raffle items... I got real and I got raw. I was desperate. And it worked! Gabe answered. A high school friend of Dennis' reached out and offered to help us. That year, Apple Valley Communications became our first sponsor. I was elated with the sponsorship and donation, but there was also a valuable lesson I learned here: People respond to heartfelt honesty!

I was pleased with my enthusiasm and the early momentum for my second chance at an event. I turned my guilt, of not knowing how to handle year one, into energy to make year two amazing! I also wanted to share more about Jocelyn and the world through her eyes. And share with our guests what day to day life looks like for her. I captured the "A day in the life of Jocelyn," homemade video and played it to the soundtrack of her favorite movie that year: Disney's Tangled (R)

The significance of Jocelyn liking Tangled was understandable in so many ways. Firstly, she was 4 years old and it was appropriate for her age to like this new craze Disney (R) movie. She was like other kids her age and I couldn't have been more proud. We would turn the movie on for her to watch if we had something to do and we couldn't give her our undivided attention; like cook dinner. Jocelyn would giggle and giggle when it turned on, while Rylee bounced her little knees, doing baby squats to the music. We were happy that they were happy and entertained for a moment. It wa also something both my girls could enjoy with other girls their age. It melted my heart and finally made me feel included, as a parent.

Slowly, I started to enjoy being around other kids again. My hatred which stemmed from envy for "typical" children began to fade. I was now more passionate to show the world how similar Jocelyn was to other children, while acknowledging the limitations Rett Syndrome left her with. I was even ready to share Jocelyn with other kids. My drive was to teach them about her, so they'd know how to interact and play with her. I encouraged the committee to involve their own children with Jocelyn's Journey. They even helped me with that year's video. With my track record of flighty emotions, I was, surprisingly, having fun!

But one evening, I paid more attention to the storyline of Tangeled. It was amazingly relatable to Jocelyn. While Rapunzel was locked and trapped in a tower by the evil stepmother, Jocelyn was locked and trapped in her own body by the evil Rett Beast! During the exciting part of the movie (when Rapunzel broke out of the tower and found freedom) I realized the significance of the movie and how Jocelyn may be relating to it. I would watch it with her and we'd both get excited when Rapunzel broke free, just like Jocelyn would one day!

I wanted to incorporate the movie, somehow, during our Jocelyn's Journey event and make it special for Jocelyn. Thank goodness our committee grew to a creative group. I could have ideas all day, but the committee members were the ones that would help design a plan in order to make my ideas happen. We had two balloons with LED lights in them on each table. We left a poem on the table with the balloons and these instructions for our guests:

> After a lil dance,
> After a lil bite,
> It'll be time for Jo and Ry
> to go "sleepy ni-night".
>
> Please help us say "goodnight"
> so they can rest their pretty heads
> by releasing your flying lantern
> as they pass by on their way to bed.

Year one, Jocelyn and Rylee disappeared after dinner and didn't really say goodbye to anyone. I felt this was a nice way for the girls to exit and for our guests to say goodbye. By the end of dinner at the gala, it would've been the girl's bedtime so it was best to have someone take them home and put them to bed. Not only that, but I didn't want Jocelyn to hear our speech. To see everyone crying, including Dennis and I. I wanted the girls to see Jocelyn's Journey as a fun party, filled with hope and love, not a time to cry over circumstances.

The day before the event, myself and Amy (a fellow committee member) were in my home office, scrambling to print the last of the brochures while Dennis was in the living room with Jocelyn and Rylee. He didn't dare come in the office, as, admittedly so, I turn into a bit of a "Bridezilla" the week of the event. So when the door opened and Dennis was holding Jocelyn's little body, it startled me.

"Jocelyn just had a seizure," was all Dennis could mutter.

"Okay," I said as my heart rate doubled and I tried not to panic. Yes, I'm an emergency room RN, but my home is not an ER! I have no suction, no oxygen, no IV, no medications, no doctor to call to bedside to give me orders on what to do. Seizures are common for Rett girls; over 80% have them. We've always known this, but when it happens, I don't care how much medical background a parent has, when it's your child, it is terrifying!

"Lay her down," I suggested as Dennis and I stared at each other with "deer in the headlight" looks.

"Her color's good," he pointed out as we watched her breathing rapidly while in a deep sleep.

"How long did it last? Was it her whole body? Did she turn blue? What happened?"

Dennis answered all of my assessment questions while we decided what to do. Once she woke up, she acted completely normal. We watched her like a hawk for the next few hours. Her behavior continued to remain normal for the rest of the day and evening. "Welp," Dennis explained calmly, "we knew this was a part of Rett. We will just keep watching her and we'll call the neurologist on Monday."

Deep down, once again, he irritated me with how calm he was, even though, I knew how upset he must have been; witnessing his daughter's first seizure. But he wasn't going to let that show. I strived to mimic his strength and calmness. But my mind raced uncontrollably, *This? THIS? A SEIZURE?! Her FIRST seizure? The night before our event?!* I was mad, but somehow empowered. I felt resistance from the Rett Beast, like something was trying to derail me from doing something huge! I was on the verge of winning and the Rett Beast felt it, so it had struck back. But it struck my daughter! I was ready, more than ever, for tomorrow night to come. Was I scared for my daughter? Yes! But Jocelyn's Journey was my only ammunition against ultimately defeating the Rett Beast and I wasn't going to back down or cancel!

September 15, 2012 was the 2nd Jocelyn's Journey gala. Yes, it was Rylee's 2nd birthday and it broke my heart to have the event on this day, but it was the only available venue date for that fall. She had a big birthday party the week before and I asked the committee to promise me, never to tell Rylee, and they agreed. 300 people came that year and we raised $49,000. Again, people were amazed at the amount of support our event received in our community. It was less than the previous year, but it was $49,000 more RSRT received than if we decided to not have an event. We had over 40 raffle baskets ranging in value from $200-$400 each! So even if some of the community wasn't physically there, they were still supporting with donations. It was an incredible sight to see, so many people coming together to cure disease! Yes, Marjorie and many high school kids prepared and served dinner, again! This was one of my favorite things, both years- selfless high school kids helping out! I was so appreciative for the help, but admired their maturity at their age.

Again, I was confused when people said it was an inspiring event. I was happy to hear this, but honestly, deep down, I didn't understand. It was sad, it was my baby. I just couldn't see how our pain was inspiring others. Hope for a cure, yes- that was obvious. But the day to day was painful, not inspiring. I was happy for the complement and just went with it.

The events of the day before, Dennis and I kept to ourselves. We stood in front of everyone again, and spoke of the daily trials we faced with having a Rett child, but we didn't breathe a word of seizures. It wasn't in the written speech, we didn't rehearse it, and it was still too fresh and painful to share with 300 people. In our speech, I strived to not appear to be complaining about our daughter. We loved her so much and we never wanted her to feel that she wasn't an important part of this family. We, again, stood in front of the mic, cried and talked about Jo, then pleaded for help to fund her cure. I may have not understood it completely, but it worked. We helped RSRT again, and I was sure there were to be blessings in that. I hoped for an expedited cure resulting from our willingness to help. As if we earned it! I was now anticipating a breakthrough, a phone call… "We've got it, Beth! We've cured it and Jocelyn will be talking and walking by Christmas!" This was my daily daydream and prayer.

The four days following the event, our family was on "honeymoon" mode. Lounging in the house, relaxing, focusing on the girls. Jocelyn didn't have another seizure in those few days, so we had hoped it was a one time thing. But just in case, I did warn her aids at preschool about what had happened.

Wednesday at 11am, her aid called me, "Beth, I think Jocelyn had a seizure. Do you want me to call 9-1-1?"

"Is she breathing?" I demanded.

"Yes."

"Is she blue?"

"No. She's just sleeping."

"No, don't call 9-1-1. I'll be right there." As I drove 80mph down the street, I honestly doubted she had had a seizure. She had been fine for the past four days and now that I warned the aids to watch for it, I figured the aid just got a little excited about something small and called it a seizure. I've seen seizing kids come into the ER by ambulance and they sometimes intubate them because they keep seizing, and I just didn't want that, without me being there to agree to it. Jocelyn was known to do some pretty weird "neuro" things that look like seizures, but when captured on a 24 hour EEG, over the summer, no seizures were noted.

When I arrived to the school, Jocelyn was awake, but groggy, tired looking. I thanked the aid and the teacher. The principal glared at me when I picked her up, "You know, we do not have a seizure care plan on file for her, we didn't know she had seizures!"

"Yeah, neither did I" I snapped back. "You'll have what you need when I decide to send her back to school," I barked as I walked out the door.

I took Jo home and placed her in her bed and she fell fast asleep. This was weird for her, she usually only took naps when she was snuggled on Dennis or I. *Maybe she did have a seizure and now she's post-dictal. My post seizure patients in the ER are out of it and sleeping for a while,* I thought.

The longest 30 minutes went by; again, odd for Jo. She didn't usually nap that long this time of day, especially when in her bed. I sat in a chair next to Jocelyn's room in our unusually silent house. Then I heard an odd groan. I peered into her room and found her on her side. I had to walk around her bed to see her face.

She was not breathing, her eyes were rolled back and her face was blue.

I scooped her up and took her to the entry way. She started to gasp as I ran for the phone and called 9-1-1. Her color returned a little and white froth came out of her mouth. Thank GOD I had asked insurance for a suction machine, the month before to use when I brush her teeth! I ran to the bathroom and grabbed it and suctioned her. Her stiff body finally loosened, her color returned, her pulse was 150 and her breathing was rapid. She was sleeping again.

The ambulance arrived and I knew the paramedics. The fire chief is our neighbor, and he heard the call go out so he came right over as well. I was so grateful the seizure had stopped. I was grateful I had back up for decision making. Mine and Dennis' co-workers were seeing me at my emotionally worst, but I was extremely grateful that I at least had taken a shower and was dressed. I can't even remember who called Dennis, who was on duty that day, but he beat us to the hospital. I absolutely hated being on the other side of healthcare, but I was so happy for our fire family and emergency services family to be right there in my hell with us that day.

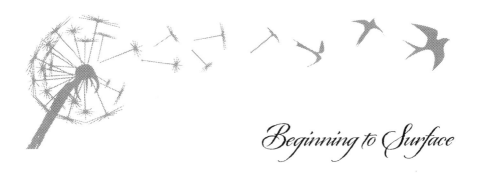

One afternoon, in January 2013, it was a strangely warm Southern California day, around 75 degrees, we were taking full advantage as a family and enjoying it. While Dennis and I were barbecuing and snacking on guacamole and chips, the girls were playing, swinging on the swing set; Jo was practicing in her "gait-trainer". We were enjoying the afternoon as a family. I felt the timing was right to bring up something to Dennis that had been on my mind for almost a month.

"Hey babe, over the last week I've counted several times that Jocelyn has been going over 17 hours without peeing."

"Really? Okay, we just need to get more in her," he replied matter of factly.

"I've been trying, Dennis, but she just spits up anything extra. I don't think she can do it."

Silence as he twiddled with the food on the grill.

"Remember how when she was first diagnosed, the neurologist said that anything out of homeostasis could trigger a seizure: 'If she's too hot, if she's too cold, if she gets sick, if she is dehydrated, if she has a fever... ANYTHING can trigger it'".

More silence.

I continued, "I'm thinking maybe she is dehydrated and that could be what triggered her having seizures. I'm happy she has been seizure free for months now, but I don't like her being on medication. What if we fixed her hydration status and then maybe that will stop the seizures too?"

"And how do we do that, Beth?" he snapped. I could tell this wasn't going as I had hoped. But I couldn't stop now.

"I think it's time to talk about a feeding tube," I managed to get out despite the lump in my throat.

"Beth, Beth Beth Beth BETH!" he exclaimed as he usually does when I am annoying him or he thinks I'm coming up with the craziest idea imaginable.

"Dennis, I don't like it either. But I cannot ignore what's going on here. 17 hours of not urinating! It's 75 degrees outside today, in January. I'm worried if we do not address this now, she wont survive the dessert heat this summer with being so dehydrated," I attempted to softly explain.

"Are you telling me, that you think our daughter is going to DIE this summer if she doesn't get a G-tube?!" All hell broke loose on the back porch.

"Yes, Dennis, I am very concerned that if we do not fix her hydration that that is a possibility," I sternly explained defensively.

He threw the spatula inside the hot barbecue and stormed into the house. I wiped tears but sighed with relief. *At least he knows what I'm thinking now,* I told myself. We didn't speak to each other for a week after that.

In February we all went to Los Angeles, where Jocelyn's neurologist is located, for a consultation with a gastrointestinal (GI) doctor, about feeding tube placement. The new complication of Jocelyn having seizures made surgery even more nerve wracking for me. I preferred the procedure to be close to her neurologist- she knew her, she listened to me and was the one specialist who actually diagnosed Jocelyn with Rett Syndrome. I just thought it was the best for Jocelyn. Tension was thick in the room as I explained the concerning details to the GI doctor, just as I had to Dennis on the back porch a few weeks prior. In the middle of my explanation of concerns to the GI doctor, he chuckled then turned to Dennis, who was holding Jocelyn.

"Okay, well let's hear from you, Dad. Sometimes moms tend to over exaggerate the truth. What's the longest Jocelyn has gone without urinating?" This doctor whom we've never met was talking about me as if I wasn't in the room!

"Like my wife said, 17 hours" Dennis calmly answered.

"And do you feel she eats like a typical 4 year old? Does it REALLY take 45 minutes to feed her a meal, like mom said?" the doctor continued with Dennis.

"Yes, at least 45 minutes. She does not eat like our friends kids who are around the same age," Dennis confirmed.

"Ohhh," the doctor replied, almost shocked that Dennis didn't join his attack on my "story". "Well, I just have to check. Moms tend to talk and make things seem worse than they really are. Dad, you said you are gone at work a lot and that leaves mom home to care for the baby and she may sometimes complain and exaggerate things to get your attention. Just watch for that."

Dennis was silent. I was in shock with the doctor, but I was so grateful for Dennis having my back, despite our silent treatment towards each other the previous few weeks. In the 15 minute visit, he prejudged and labeled me, with some of the worst I had to date: exaggerator, attention seeker, liar, and worst of all: Munchausen's by Proxy Syndrome. Munchausen's is a psychological condition where a caregiver, or parent, intentionally causes harm to a child. Have you seen the movie "Sixth Sense" where the little boy who sees dead people helps the ghost girl show her dad the video of her mom poisoning her? THAT is Munchausen's! It is serious and deadly! And THAT is what this doctor was getting at! I know how to look for Munchausen's-, I'm an RN! I knew what this doctor thought of me. We left that office and never returned.

Thankfully, the next day we were able to get in to see Jocelyn's original GI doctor, though not at the same facility as her neurologist. After the first GI doctor consultation, I was a little nervous about the second, but this doctor empathetically listened to my concerns and agreed, that it was time for a g-tube, now before things got worse. He also pointed out that Jocelyn was still considered "FAILURE to thrive". I was annoyed that he just had to throw that in there, but quickly swallowed my pride. On a positive note, they would fix her reflux during the g-tube placement so Jocelyn wouldn't spit up anymore. It was called a "nissen fundoplication"- they wrap the top of her stomach around the bottom of the esophagus and put a stitch in it to prevent regurgitation. That sounded great- no more spit ups, still, it was hard to be positive. It was a 5 year battle Dennis and

I fought to get weight on her, keep weight on her, and to make sure she got enough fluid so her "pluming" wouldn't get backed up. A g-tube could help all of that. Still, we felt like we were giving up and waving a white flag. We kept our decision to move forward with the g-tube to ourselves, and only told immediate family, until right before the date of the surgery.

During that time, friends and family were urging me to start planning the 2013 Jocelyn's Journey event. I knew if we were to have a 2013 event, it was going to be a hard one. Jocelyn's condition was changing having seizures last year, the seizure medication side effects, her scoliosis had worsened to the point that we needed to put her in a back brace, and now a g-tube in her future. Meanwhile, Dennis and I were striving to keep our family together and as normal as possible. So planning and organizing an event and monthly committee meetings just seemed a little much. My mom offered to do all the heavy lifting for the event if we decided to have one. I would be a committee member who was in charge of a slide show and speech the night of the event. I decided to give her the reins to the committee and the planning began.

The weeks before Jocelyn's surgery were tense around the house. Dennis and I hardly spoke. There was little laughter unless the kids were being silly. We were scared. We were worried. Finally, the Friday before the surgery date, I posted what was about to happen on Facebook and asked for prayers. I didn't want to call each family member. I didn't want to answer questions and explain everything over and over again. I just wanted to say it one time...

> It's hard enough being a parent, let alone a special needs parent. We've made the difficult decision to have a feeding tube placed for our Baby Jo and surgically fix her reflux MONDAY! We've been fighting the inevitable for years and know that it is now time. Dennis and I are nervous, to say the least, but remain very optimistic and honest with Jocelyn and Rylee. The procedure is at 1200 Monday at Kaiser, Fontana, and we'd appreciate positive thoughts and prayers! Jo will then go to PICU and spend a few days in patient. I will keep everyone updated via Facebook, as it is easiest to mass broadcast. Thank you to everyone who has stepped it up to help us this week.

The outpour of support was reassuring during a time when Dennis and I felt most alone.

My nurse brain went bonkers, again! Mostly, I was worried about the anesthesia- just like when Jocelyn had her MRI. I was worried there would be a problem getting her off the ventilator (breathing machine). I never asked what Dennis was worried about. I was scared to ask. Always calm, my husband was in a silent panic and I felt responsible. When Dennis gets upset, everyone should be upset.

April 15, two weeks before Jocelyn's 5th birthday, was our surgery day. The car ride down was silent. Jo was so hungry, and ever since her birth, I have been a mama lion when it comes to my cubs being hungry. My face felt beat red and I was infuriatingly helpless to not be able to give Jocelyn a basic need. I wanted to throw up! I could tell she was confused as to why we were not providing for her. We were running late on top of everything else, so Dennis decided to drop Jocelyn and I at the hospital doors, while he searched the parking structure for a parking spot.

Pre-op registration was horrible, and it seemed to be taking forever for the nurses to call us back to start an IV on Jocelyn. I, unrealistically, wanted her IV started right when we pulled up. I wanted to get my, already thin, dehydrated, now hungry daughter some fluid and sugar in her body. *I know too much. I know too much,* I kept telling myself in attempts to reassure my thoughts and shut them up. In the midst of my silent, internal, battle of worry, my cell phone started to play music from the internet station we were listening to on the car ride to the hospital. I thought it was odd, having not played anything for over 15 minutes and now, all of a sudden it starts playing. Then I noticed the song... it was "Look After You" by The Frey. I knew the song, but at that moment, as I was listening to the words, I couldn't help but feel that the timing for it playing, right in that moment, something was trying to tell me something:

> If I don't say this now I will surely break
> As I'm leaving the one I want to take
> Forget the urgency but hurry up and wait
> My heart has started to separate.

There now, steady love, so few come and don't go
Will you, won't you be the one I'll always know?
When I'm losing my control, the city spins around
You're the only one who knows, you slow it down.

The lyrics penetrated me so deep, all I could do was cry in the crowded waiting room. I didn't care what stranger noticed me. I was, however, grateful that Dennis wasn't with us yet, as I wanted a moment alone with my daughter. I realized I wasn't prepared for the worst. I knew what my "worst case scenario" fear was, but I was not prepared for it. I held Jocelyn and looked her in the eyes and smiled so it looked like happy tears to her. I tightly rocked her to the song and prepared for the worst possible outcome. And right then and there, I said goodbye to my daughter.

"Jocelyn Emily, you are the most amazing thing that has ever happened to me. Daddy and I love you so much and you make this world a better place. Your infectious smile and laughter brightens the worst of days. We are so blessed to be your parents. We love you so much and no matter what happens, everything is going to be okay, I promise. I know you are tired and hungry right now, but soon, you wont be, I promise. We are having the doctors help us help you to eat more. So you get stronger. It might be a little scary. I'm scared too. But we just have to say our prayers and be strong. Daddy and I love you so much and we always will! You are the first, best thing that has ever happened to us, never forget that!"

Jocelyn seemed to take in every word. She was calm and quiet, rocking peacefully in my arms as the song continued. Dennis came in right when Jocelyn and I were done with our "heart to heart". He was embarrassed at my loud cell phone in the waiting room.

"Turn that off, Beth. What's wrong, why are you crying?!"

"I'm fine," I quickly snapped at him. I handed Jocelyn off to her Daddy and instructed him, "You need to hold her and snuggle her for a while." He obliged without question. I left the room to walk to an adjacent hall way to dry my eyes and turn off the mysterious cell phone music.

Finally, we were called back to a curtained room with a crib in it. Jocelyn laid quietly as they started her IV then, fell asleep. I was immediately relieved and felt better that she was getting some sugar in her. *She must have felt horrible, maybe even had a headache from being hungry.*

My empathy for my daughter was fading with every drop of the fluid into the chamber, into the tube, then down her little arm. Jocelyn looked frail to me, and pale. I tried to remain positive. I put a flower in her hair, like I always do when she goes out in public. "We're lucky her flower matches her gown," I broke the ice with Dennis. It got a smirk and an eye roll out of him and I was pleased with myself for the comment, and the flower!

Then, 30 minutes after the scheduled OR time, two nurses threw the pre-op curtain open and said, "Okay, it's time," as they unlocked the wheels to Jo's oversized metal crib. We each quickly gave her one last kiss. I smiled at her and fought tears and told her I'd see her in a minute. We followed them as far as we could, then at the forbidden red line on the ground, the nurses turned, smiled and waved bye to us. Now the tears came, as well as sweat and nausea. The clock was ticking... The lyrics from the song started playing in my head:

> *As I'm leaving the one I want to take*
> *Forget the urgency but hurry up and wait*
> *My heart has started to separate*

In the waiting room, Dennis and I decided to eat. It was all we could do to stay busy in a waiting room. We small talked over sandwiches while a small TV played the news. My sandwich quickly created a stomach ache as I started to pay attention to the news. There was a bombing in Boston during a marathon. *What is wrong with the world?* I thought. *There is already so much hurt and pain in the world and then people want to kill each other, for no reason!* I left the room. I couldn't handle anymore death, injury or ugliness.

While walking the halls near the waiting room, staying close enough to hear someone call us if needed, I noticed what a horrible room this was to be in. Many, many family members waiting for news on their loved one. They all probably had the same nauseating knot in their stomach as I did. It was the realist place I've ever been I realized. *I hate being on the other side of healthcare,* I thought for the thousandth time.

The Frey began to play again in my head on my walk:
There now, steady love, so few come and don't go

Will you, won't you be the one I'll always know?
When I'm losing my control, the city spins around
You're the only one who knows, you slow it down

Losing control was right. I was not in control at all! I wasn't with Jocelyn, I had no idea how the procedure was going. I was helpless and that made me so uncomfortable. I began pacing. Ignoring my surroundings, my thoughts turned to God. I knew He was the only thing in control. I admitted to Him that I hadn't been coping well, the past few years. I knew I had put my family through a lot. Jocelyn's therapy and Jocelyn's Journey was the focus of my life. I wasn't being the mom I envisioned I'd be: baking cookies, going on outings, going to church. I wasn't being the wife I wanted to be: packing lunches with love letters, having weekly date nights, vacations. Dennis and I didn't talk about our future or our dreams anymore. Probably because we were terrified of the future. The rare occasion we got a babysitter for a night out, we took full advantage and partied way too hard. Never a bonding moment, just an escape, for a night, from the reality of where we had ended up. I realized in that hallway how bad I sucked! Guilt filled me. I began to realize I didn't deserve Jocelyn, Rylee or Dennis. I wasn't who I wanted to be, who I should be. What good was I to my family or to the world if I wasn't giving everyone my all? A few more lyrics from the song punched me in the gut right in the hallway.

*Oh, oh, oh, Be my Baby, I'll look after you.*

The flood gates to my eyes flew wide open, and I began to beg: *Lord, she is my baby! My baby! PLEASE let me look after her. Let me continue to look after her! I'll do better! I can do better! Let me show you! I want another chance. I promise I will take better care of Jocelyn. I promise I'll be better with Rylee too and she will love her childhood. I'm so sorry I haven't been honoring Dennis as his wife. I've been acting crazy, doing what I want, what I think is right. I can do this, Lord! Give me another chance, PLEASE! Don't take her from me! She's my baby- let me look after her, PLEASE!*

Over and over and over I begged and prayed and promised. To strangers, seeing me walk the halls, I probably looked like a psych patient talking to the voices in my head. I thought to myself, *I really need to quit looking like a crazy person walking this hospital campus.* But at the same time, I didn't care what I looked like to anyone. I was having a moment!

About two hours after they wheeled Jocelyn down the hall, a nurse called Dennis and I to the recovery room. Jocelyn looked like a breath of fresh air. Peace. I was at peace. She was peacefully sleeping. I felt like I could finally breathe. Like I was under water for an hour and had just now surfaced.

When Jocelyn finally began to wake, she was groggy from all the medication and sedation, but not uncomfortable. Once we were in the pediatric ICU she was allowed to eat a bit of jello and was able to get down a few bites before falling asleep again.

Later that night, Dennis went home and visited with Rylee, who was at my brother's house for the day. I stayed with Jocelyn and watched her and everyone else's every move. I was ready to live up to my promise- I was going to be the best at taking care of her, every second. All three nights we were in the hospital I strived to keep us on a schedule as much as possible. I gave her a sponge bath, put a new gown on her and tucked her into her hospital bed. I laid right next to her every single night. I snuggled her and held her close to me and stroked her brown hair. I prayed and thanked God for giving me a second chance. I thanked Him for letting me just hold her. The last night, in the middle of my prayer of gratitude, I reflected on the night Jocelyn was born in the very same hospital. "Just let me hold her," I had begged God during my crash c-section, uncertain if she would survive. And He did- He let me hold her. And ever since that day, I have been holding her. Tears of gratitude soaked my pillow. In that moment, I began to see a pattern with God. I felt a strong sense of purpose for Jocelyn and everything we had been through. I became a little more confident in God, that He was going to see us through these hard times and that He was listening.

By May, just one month after g-tube placement, we started to get a routine down with the tube feedings. Dennis and I were so relieved that Jocelyn would still eat solid food. "You don't use it, you loose it," we always hear in emergency services, pertaining to trainings and re-certifications. However, there was truth behind this saying in skills with Rett girls. One of Dennis and my worries with the g-tube was that Jocelyn would rely on tube feedings only, and lose the ability to swallow. By history, we knew how quickly Rett Syndrome could rob our daughter of skills. So we were very pleased that, even a month later, she could still eat and swallow food and some liquids. Things were going well and Dennis and I were starting to relax a little again and we started being nice to each other. The white elephant was finally evicted from our home!

Five days after her surgery, the doctors released Jocelyn from any limitations. They said I could put her scoliosis brace back on and start bolus feeding her, which meant that the feed was given with a large syringe; an entire feed all at once rather than the use of a pump to infuse small doses over a period of time. I didn't know how to "bolus" feed and no one in the hospital told me how. Perhaps because they found out that I was an RN, and they just expected I knew. Sure, I'd given medication through a g-tube to a patient before who had had the tube for years. But this was a "fresh" tube and I was introducing nutrition, not a little bit of medication! Thank goodness for the army of friends I have in different fields of nursing, who helped me figure out how to work Jocelyn up to this bolus feeding.

During her first bolus feed, I was careful and did exactly what my fellow RN instructed. I was almost done getting 3 ounces of formula into her and suddenly a volcano of formula erupted out of Jocelyn's mouth and nose! I felt horrible, not just because I over filled her and made her vomit, but because it probably hurt. They had surgically stitched her stomach so she wasn't supposed to vomit. I ran her into the bedroom where Dennis was, balling my eyes out. It was the same feeling as when I snipped her adorable little finger, the first time I cut her nails as an infant and we both cried and cried. She was so helpless, needing me to care for her. And while I thought I was, I messed up and hurt her. I didn't think I could ever forgive myself.

Over the next week I worked Jocelyn up to bolus feeds again, but with success this time. She was ready to go back to pre-school but I had a hard time allowing it. I knew she was tired of being at home. She loved school, the kids, her teachers… I instructed everyone prior to her first day back that they had to be careful. Everyone understood and appreciated the heads up. We really had a great team of supportive teachers and therapists at school. I was so grateful for their help and patience with us.

One morning, I was scrambling to get Jocelyn's stuff ready before the bus picked her up. I was pressed for time, trying to be gentle with Jocelyn's tube site and back brace. She was on her bed, just as she was every morning when I got her dressed. Dressing Jocelyn reminded me of dressing a stroke patient at work. You have to put your hand in the ankle part of the pants, then grab her foot and thread the pants on, one leg at a time. The same goes for the shirts… and sweaters… Sometimes I felt that a stroke patient was easier because most had completely flaccid limbs that wouldn't move. Jocelyn, on the other hand, would sometimes have her hands and legs flailing all over the place in attempts to help me. Each limb was like trying to grab a fish and pull it through the clothes to thread them on. This particular morning, while racing the clock and fishing for all 4 limbs to dress her, I was a little out of breath by the time I got to her shoes. I was getting frustrated with her scrunching up her toes, making it impossible to slide on a shoe. I got one on, then as I was struggling with the other, the first fell off. I was late, I didn't have time for this. I became infuriated.

"Are you kidding me?!" I yelled to the ceiling envisioning the heavens above. "It's shoes! It's stupid shoes! You can't give me that? I am doing my best here, we've come this far with serious things and now shoes?! Shoes?! It's just shoes!"

The flood gates opened. Rylee ran through her room, into her closet and slammed the door shut. She didn't understand why I was yelling and crying and she didn't know how to handle it. So she hid in the closet (it must be hereditary). Jocelyn laid quietly on her bed as I left her room and started throwing her shoes into the living room. I paced and ranted and screamed and ugly cried: "Where are you? 'God will only give you what you can handle'? What a load of garbage! I can't do shoes! You aren't here, I promised I would be better and I am doing my best but you have to give me a little! How am I supposed to be better and live up to that promise when you wont even help me with her shoes! Are you kidding me?! It's just shoes!"

My rant went on over and over for what seemed like 10 minutes. My eyes ran dry, I remembered that I was already running late. I went into Jocelyn's room and she remained quiet and on her bed, waiting for me. I gently put her in her wheelchair. I collected her shoes which I had thrown into the other room and slipped them right on. I kissed Jo on the head and quietly apologized for yelling. I told her she was a good girl and mommy needed a nap.

Before going out, I found the darkest pair of sunglasses and a baseball hat to hide my face. Glancing outside, I noticed the bus was waiting for us at the curb and I wheeled Jocelyn out. Rylee crept outside to join us and walked her sister to the bus, as she did every morning.

"Good morning," I told the bus driver with a cheerful pitch and a giant smile. Could *she have heard me in my rant? How long was she waiting there? Are there any windows open?*

"Good morning" she happily answered. "Hi Jocelyn. Hi Rylee," she acknowledged as she routinely did and loaded Jocelyn up. I kissed Jocelyn's head, told her she was a good girl and I loved her. The bus driver and I said our usual good bye, then Rylee followed me back into the house. As the front door closed behind us, I collapsed face first on our couch ottoman in complete exhaustion. I reflected on my friendly interaction with the bus driver. Sarcasm set in as I announced: "And the academy award goes to... Elizabeth Jones!"

*Catalyst*

Somehow, I was still holding on to my pleading promise to God: I was ready to be better. I figured it started with me, I obviously needed to figure a few things out. I had to be in a good state of health to be able to be more attentive to my family. I decided to join a Crossfit gym. It was pretty amazing. I loved the work out and the people. The "CaveMan" diet they offered was not for me. I needed quick meals and for that diet it meant sautéing. So about 2 weeks into this "diet", I ended up in the ER with a gallbladder attack. *GREAT! Another "fail" to add to my long list. I'm over it!* I thought. If I need to eat cereal for dinner because I'm a super busy mom, then that's the way it is. My trip to the ER made me realize how important it was for me to be at my best, physically. *What if something happened to me? Who would take care of Jocelyn?* My epiphany only fueled my fire to be the best me possibly, physically, mentally, and spiritually.

I continued to go to the gym, but soon realized it was too much for the girls. It interrupted nap times and feeding times. And when Jo was out of school, it would interrupt her new tube feed schedule. I suddenly felt selfish rather than "self improving". Call me a "quitter", but I had to make a decision between a gym I loved and my kids- my kids won!

I was also trying to be better with our finances at home. I didn't want to leave the girls to pick up overtime shifts, but I thought I could somehow make money while being at home with them. I laughed when I signed up for Publisher's Clearing House- hey, you never know… But no one ever showed up at my door with a giant check. All I ended up with was a silly retractable hose that continues to collect dust in the garage. Then I tried an online advertising course- yeah, epic fail.

Then my friend, Christi, told me about something called AdvoCare- a nutritional supplement company. She said she was making extra money and by taking some of their products, she lost 30 pounds. I figured I could stand to lose a few stress pounds, but I loved that this was about nutrition, not dieting. The last thing I needed was another trip to the ER because of a diet! I was also interested in the "extra money" part.

AdvoCare had been around for over 20 years, but what really intrigued me, was their Science Advisory Board, Dr Stanley Dudrick namely. He is referred to as the father of IV nutrition (Total Parenteral Nutrition, or TPN). Everything the body needs to sustain life he designed to get into the body through a vein and bypass the gut! As an RN, I knew what TPN was and had seen it a few times in the ER. It's usually found in long term care facilities, for patients who can no longer eat by mouth. I had recently heard of a few Rett girls on TPN and I instantly felt connected with Dr. Dudrick and was appreciative of his work, for my fellow Rett families.

After six months of being on AdvoCare, I lost 20 pounds. I was at my high school weight at 32 years old. I never thought that would happen. But it wasn't just the weight loss I was impressed with, it was the energy! I was finally the mom I wanted to be: crafting with the girls, make up day, baking. We even went on outings to the park, to the mall, to story time at the library. I was doing it! I was being "better", as I swore I would be! And icing on the cake, I was making money with my new, home-based business!

The products were amazing, the income was great, but there was even more AdvoCare gave me. There were training calls and seminars I attended to learn more about the product, but also about leadership. A huge lesson I walked away with at one of my first AdvoCare trainings was this: "Being happy is a choice. My thoughts create my words which create my world." Once I decided to be happy, I had to control my thoughts. Any thoughts about myself or anyone else that were mean, ugly or gave me anxious feelings, I had to immediately stop thinking them, hypothetically grab onto them, and throw them into the pit of hell where they belonged. Happy thoughts or a joke, which gave me good energy and brought peace to myself, I tightly held onto. This took a lot of practice at first. It was so easy to be negative, but I had made the decision to be happy, so I was working my hardest at it. I felt like one of those cartoon characters with an angel on one shoulder and the devil on the other. As they fought over my thoughts, I had to silence the devil character and encourage the angel to keep talking.

Once my thoughts changed, my words did. I only spoke kind words to people. When I thought of someone and it made me smile, I would call or message them and let them know I was thinking of them. I was obedient to this process and to this change. I was so tired of ugliness. Ugliness with myself, ugliness in the world… I veered away from ugliness and negativity as much as I possibly could. My thoughts were precious and I had to protect them. This was when I limited my exposure to the news. So much sadness, ugliness, embellished drama… people usually at their worst. And this was "entertainment"?! If my thoughts were creating my world, they were too precious for such things to poison them.

A few months later, at another AdvoCare gathering in San Diego, a speaker said something that rocked my world! She said, "Your children will do what you do. Be the example." I was much better off than where I was the year before, but I still had areas that I wanted to improve. I thanked God for Jocelyn, Rylee… my family. I made a promise to Him that I would be better and I truly felt I was well on my way to becoming better. However, my girls didn't see me do any of it! *Your children will do what you do*, echoed in my head. I then realized, my girls needed to see me be better. See me pray, so they would also pray.

The next day when I got home, I decided we were going to pray before dinner. (Regrettably, something we never had done before unless we were at our parents home.) Three year old Rylee adamantly refused. "I don't want to."

"Rylee," I pleaded, "we need to thank Jesus for everything He's done for us."

Not knowing what she was saying, she replied, "I don't want to. I don't like Jesus!"

My heart broke right then and there. I wanted so badly to punish her, but I knew it wasn't her fault, it was mine! *Your children will do what you do*, continued to echo in my head the rest of the week. It was time to fix this. It was time to take action! We were in need of a church with a children's ministry and we needed it NOW!

I remembered my long time friend and hairdresser, Ginny, telling me about her church. She was always so excited about how her two young children loved going, and how her and her husband had grown closer since attending. I wanted that! All of it! I texted her that night and asked what time services were.

That Sunday the girls and I arrived 30 minutes before service started. As we hung out in the lobby, I first noticed Vinnie. I had known Vinnie when I was in high school. We worked together at a local drug store. Vinnie had always been a "good guy," where I had been a self absorbed teenager. I remember one day at the drug store, in particular. Vinnie was just getting off his lunch break and I was about to start mine. As we crossed paths, he was frantically searching for something in the break room. I thought he had lost his wallet, keys, or something he couldn't function without.

"What's wrong Vinnie?" I asked concerned.

"I can't find my bible" he explained in a panic. I honestly chuckled to myself, relieved it wasn't anything important. He continued, "It's my favorite one. I left it right here on the table as I dozed on the couch for a minute. Now I can't find it."

"Oh, I'm sorry Vinnie," I said sympathetically, as I walked passed him on my way out to lunch. *Weird,* I thought to myself. Then I remembered in conversation once, Vinnie told me he wanted to go to school to be a pastor after high school. *Well, it's important to him,* I thought, thinking of the lost bible.

About an hour later, I returned to the break room from my lunch break. Vinnie was still looking in and out of the break room, hoping to find his lost treasure.

"Did you find it?" I asked.

"No" he said sadly. "But why would someone take my bible?" he asked himself out loud. "Well, I guess they needed it more than me," he concluded and instantly got over it and went back out to work. That forever left an impression on me. Such a mature thought process for a high schooler, which left me embarrassed for my secret, immature chuckle about the whole ordeal. *Maybe he knows something I don't,* I wondered for a brief second, then carried on with my day without ever thinking about it again. Until now.

"HI BETH!" Vinnie approached me in the lobby of the church as I was snapping out of my day dream. "How are you?"

"Hi Vinnie, I am good! These are my girls. We wanted to come check out the church today," I answered.

"That's awesome. So how've you been? What do you do? Are you married?" He sat down at a table across from me and I was shocked that he was taking the time to sit and chat before service. He was kind and genuinely interested. I told him about Dennis and how I'm an RN and now I do AdvoCare from home.

"What's AdvoCare?" he asked. I wanted to explain how it changed my life and made me a more positive person. How the most recent event in San Diego has lead me on this quest for a good church which was what brought me there today.

"It's a sports nutrition company, but with the most positive people I've ever met. And I love it and it's what led me to come here and grow in my faith." I "firehosed" poor Vinnie. He was so polite and kind, even though I probably made little sense to him.

"Wow, Beth. That sounds like an amazing company. I'm happy for you."

I felt like an idiot for a minute, but then we started chatting about Vinnie and his wife and kids. He then told me he was the lead pastor there! He had done it! He knew what he wanted way back in high school and he was living it! I was so happy for him, then suddenly star struck, that he was taking the time to sit and talk with me for so long, right before service. He made me feel so welcomed and comfortable. Changing churches can be a bit overwhelming but he absolutely eased my anxiety. I felt relaxed, welcomed and right at home. What I probably loved the most was that he acknowledged my girls. Conversed with Rylee, and then spoke directly to Jocelyn to engage with her. He didn't tap dance around the fact that Jocelyn was in a wheel chair. He directly asked what her disability was. I appreciated this and gave a two minute education on Rett Syndrome. He listened intently then said he would pray for her and her cure. I was touched!

"Okay Beth," he politely ended the conversation. "Well, hopefully I'll meet your husband next time as well," he mentioned as he pushed his chair in and went to help someone prepare for the service.

"Yeah, that would be awesome. Maybe soon." Dennis was more than okay with us girls going to church, but he was working a lot of Sundays and wasn't able to join us. And I couldn't wait for us to go all together, as a family. I couldn't wait for anything or anyone! My girls needed Jesus, and stat!

We continued to go to Pastor Vinnie's church, and after a few months, both me and the girls were enjoying it, and were learning so much! One day, my heart filled with satisfaction as 3 year old Rylee approached me and educated me, "Mommy, Jesus is in my heart!" Done! Tears of joy filled my eyes. Just in a few short months of going to this church, Rylee was talking with love for Jesus. WIN! I made the right decision, finally!

During service, Rylee would be in the children's classroom learning at her level, while I kept Jocelyn with me. Jocelyn was a handful I was willing to endure during service. She would usually snuggle up on me and nap. When she woke I would immediately shove snacks in her mouth to keep her mouth busy eating instead of making noises. When it was time for worship music, Jocelyn would stand with my support and watch the words on the big screen (a reinforcer for teaching her to read- I was double pleased). During the music, I would let her yell and "sing" as loud as she wanted and no one around seemed to mind. They would giggle at her voisterousness, as would I.

One day, Rylee came out of her bedroom singing a song she was making up as she went along: "Jesus.... loves me... he likes when I clean my room... Jesus loves Sissy.... lalalala..." Dennis looked at me and raised an eyebrow and we both chuckled at our daughter.

"You turned her into a bible thumper!"

"Thank you!" I replied proudly.

What I liked most about Pastor Vinnie, and all the leaders at church, was that they taught and preached directly from the bible. "Don't take my word for it" they'd say, "go look it up in your bible!" I was so happy I had my bible and even more grateful that I knew how to use it. My older brother had taught me... while he was incarcerated! I remember he used to sign my letters and have bible verses at the end of them. One time, I finally found the courage to tell him in a reply letter that I had no idea what it all meant: "John 14: 1-7". He graciously explained it all in his next letter and he too, admitted, that he had never knew how, either, until someone he met in jail taught him. This chain of events, just proves, there is something to be learned by everyone. I also then realized, even a person isolated to the extreme, can still make a difference in the world, if he or she chooses to do so.

The spring of 2014, Crystal Gax invited me to a women's weekend retreat she'd learned about through her work. She was hesitant or nervous to go and it felt like she wanted someone to go with her for support. Absolutely! I was more than excited to go.

The retreat was in the nearby mountains, in an oversized cabin, which had, maybe, 7 rooms. About 25 women were present, with 5 leaders. It was so incredible to wear yoga pants, no make up and be around women of all walks of life; each having their own experience with God.

The second night we were there, we talked about "false idols". I had always thought false idols were the standard: money, cars, purses, designer clothes… things you worship that weren't necessary or that are "worldly". That weekend, my definition of false idols expanded. One of the leaders explained it to me as anything that preoccupies your time. Thoughts and energy which prevents you from keeping your time, thoughts and energy on God.

It was so thoughtful the way the leaders set up that evening. We were to write down our individual "false idols" on dissolvable paper, pray over them then put them in water to let them go. Everyone around me seemed to do this quickly. They knew what their false idol was. I couldn't think of anything. I like my home, but if I lost it, it wouldn't be the end of the world- we would get through it. I hated shopping, especially after having Jocelyn, because I thought it was such a waste of money to spend money that could go to research to cure Rett, or any other disease for that matter.

I sat at my table and I was the last person who still had nothing written on my paper. I worried the other women would think that I was self righteous and that I thought I had no false idols and that I was perfect. I sat there, not wanting to just move on, I just needed to understand.

Finally, one of the leaders sat with me. I started to cry. I knew I needed help and that I just couldn't figure this exercise out. The sweet lady saw my empty paper and asked, "What do you live for every day? What do you eat, breath, think of? What takes up all of your time and your thoughts and your energy?"

"Well, my kids, but that's it," I admitted, feeling like I had no life and that I was "one of those moms".

"Well then write their names down, and let them go," she replied simply.

"Never!" I defended. "Those are my kids, if I don't do what I do, then how will they know they are loved? Without all my efforts, how would they be successful in life? And with Jocelyn, with everything I have to do for her, how would she survive if I just 'let her go?'"

"Okay," the sweet lady replied gently as she knew she was treading on a very sensitive subject for me. "Ask yourself this: Do you think that you could do a better job with your children than all healing, miracle working, forever perfect, God?" Her words punched me directly in my heart. I got it, I finally understood. My sweet little tears turned into a snotty, ugly cry. She sat there with me, with one arm around me, until I could finally speak.

"But I don't want to give them to Him. They are mine," I knew how self righteous I was being now, but I didn't care. I always believed that I knew what was best for them because I was their Mommy! I was always told that I was their best advocate!

"Then don't do it now. Just know, they've always belonged to Him. But, if you want to have a closer relationship with Jesus and live the life He created you for, you need to let go of false idols." She softly walked away, and I continued to ugly cry through a box of tissue.

After that conversation, I knew I was going to do this, tonight. I just needed a minute. Finally with a shakey hand, I wrote "Jocelyn, Rylee, Jocelyn's Journey, Cure for Rett". I walked into the next room where the rest of the women were surrounded by a bowl of water. I put my paper in the bowl of water and watched my paper with my list on it, slowly disappear. I wasn't regretful, I was relieved it was over. Then, peace fell over me.

The moment I left the retreat and got off that mountain, I was in full swing practice of living a false idol-less life. I consulted with God about everything. If I was going to be who God designed me to be, I needed His help every step of the way. When faced with a decision, I prayed about it and included Him. It was definitely a practiced art, just like the decision to be happy. But I soon realized, that this is how God designed us- to rely on Him for everything, and trust that He will see us through everything.

The second night I was home brought a large dose of adversity- trying to throw me off of this new practice I was living by. At 2am I heard Jocelyn moaning. The past few months, she wasn't sleeping that great at night because of Rett, but she would usually babble or giggle and I would turn the monitor off and go back to sleep. But this night was different. A moan, something wasn't right.

I walked in her room and found her completely soaked and all of her bedding completely drenched. I found the tubing from her night feed, dislodged from her abdomen and feeding her bed. From the smell of partially digested formula in her hair and all over her neck, I could tell she vomited. Again, she wasn't supposed to be able to vomit! I very calmly stripped her down and put her into a warm bath. Her body was freezing and my eyes filled with tears, wondering how long she was laying like this in bed. I replaced my guilt with "Thank you God, that I heard her!"

Once she was clean and had new clean sheets, I laid her back in bed and she snuggled right down and was fast asleep- exhausted from all the commotion. I gave her a kiss, smirked, and told God, "Welp, she's all yours! What do you want me to do about this?" There was such peace in me, which was strange when something wrong happened, especially with Jo. I giggled to myself, thinking of how I would've reacted a week ago, freaking out that she was hypothermic or that she had aspirated… which very well could've happened. But somehow, I was confident that if any of those horrible things were the case, God would let me know. Just like He made sure I woke to her little moan.

The next morning I went to the drawing board with what to do. Consulting with God, I sat and thought and prayed for a while before acting. I had been wanting Jocelyn off night feeds for a while now. Normal "guts" have a period of rest- Jocelyn's should too. I had also wanted to get her off of formula, understanding that there were so many hormones in milk derivatives. The hormones in food and milk worried me for my whole family, but especially for Jocelyn. I learned, on a Rett support group social media page, that girls with Rett, or any neurological disorder, can go into puberty at an extremely early age. If I could help prevent that from happening by eliminating hormones as much as I could, I was going to do it.

Kelly came to mind. She was a Rett mom I met on social media and I knew she made her daughter's tube feeds by hand. I immediately messaged her and she sent me over her feeding schedule as well as what she mixed for her daughter, in order to ensure there was enough calories, protein and other nutrients. I took her advice because it just made sense. Advice from a fellow Rett mom was better than any given by Jocelyn's doctors because it was someone who actually lived and understood what I needed help with and why. I was so appreciative of Kelly.

Unfortunately, the blender I had wasn't the kind Kelly used. Mine wouldn't finely chop the food like Kelly's did. The blended mixture kept getting stuck in the tubes connected to Jocelyn as I was trying to feed her. Once clogged, the tubing was trash, waisting our precious supplies. I only had room for error occasionally, because insurance would only send a certain number of feed bags per month. I didn't give up though. I didn't get anxious either. I just sat and prayed and waited for the big man to give me some answers.

The next morning I was mixing my favorite flavor of AdvoCare shake, as I do every morning. Then, I had a thought. I am now in the best of health I've ever been in with incredible energy. Why don't I give Jocelyn a shake?! I checked the ingredients out first, they had enough protein for her entire day, incredible fiber, which most Rett girls are in desperate need of, and it was made by the best of the best- Dr Dudrick! I mixed it with warm water, threw it in the blender and it worked! It didn't clog in the pump. It was fantastic! BOOM! *Thank you God, for putting that thought in my head!*

The next few days I added a few other AdvoCare products including Rehydrate, Omegas, Probiotic and FiboTrim. I don't know why I was so surprised with the results in Jocelyn- I knew how good AdvoCare felt! She started sleeping through the night, which was great, but the best part, her poops. She was having "Advo-poops"! (If you can't talk about poop, you probably won't be successful at AdvoCare, and you probably don't have a Rett child.) Jocelyn could go potty without it hurting. "Nuggets" were a thing of the past! It was hard to believe that just a month prior, we were battling constipation and using extreme measures to get her to go! Now she would go, lickedy split, no problem. This is HUGE for any Rett parent. To watch your child in such discomfort, sometimes screaming because of gas or constipation is too much to bare. But now, she was Advo-pooping! I was thrilled!

Within the first year of Jocelyn being tube fed with formula and water, she gained 3 pounds. We were pretty pleased with that, and happy she was getting hydrated more than what we could accomplish with oral. However, being on AdvoCare products, getting things flowing appropriately, decreasing her stomach aches so she was actually wanting to eat more food, it took just 3 short months for Jocelyn to gain 7 pounds! This all started 2 days after I gave my children to God on that mountain. If there was any doubt, this was obvious confirmation that God could do much better than what I was doing. *Thank you GOD!*

I know now that all along my "Mommy instincts," or "gut feelings" with my children had always been God telling me what to do. He is my children's best advocate, not me! They are His, I just pray for direction and discernment on what He wants me to do. He gets the credit and the glory, not me.

*Speak It!*

During my adventure with AdvoCare, Dennis was working extra shifts at the fire station. It was too hard to find a sitter every time I had to go in for a 12 hour shift. It's hard to find someone willing to take care of Jocelyn with all her needs, then add Rylee to the mix, with her 3 year old demands as well. So I took a leave of absence from work and continued with AdvoCare in the cracks of my time. We were staying afloat and on Dennis' days off, we were a family of 4 spending time together. This rarely happened when we were both working and we were really starting to enjoy this!

We were a week away from seeing over 200 of our family, friends, and community at the 3rd Jocelyn's Journey Gala. Dennis was exhausted from work, so I relinquished him of speaking that year and I stood alone during my speech. Some people questioned why Dennis didn't speak and why I stood up in front alone. I simply stated that he was too tired. The truth was, it broke my heart to see him break down every year in front of everyone. I was a bit defensive of my husband and if he wanted to sit a year out, I was okay with that, despite the critics.

October 20, 2013, Jocelyn's Journey event theme was "Be Brave," which was very appropriate given the events from the last year. I felt we were brave having an event in the first place, let alone getting a G-tube, starting a home-based business, and our decision for me to take a leave of absence and stay home with the girls. In the spirit of being brave, I didn't read from a speech- I just spoke to our guests from an outline. This took a lot of practice and a lot of prayer. But, remember, "Jocelyn's Journey" was also written on my list of false idols on my dissolvable paper. I gave

"Jocelyn's Journey" to God. It was His, not mine. With His track record with Jocelyn's feeds over the last few months and her now thriving, I was filled with faith that He would make "Jocelyn's Journey" also thrive. I no longer owned "Jocelyn's Journey", I was simple an obedient person in the process.

I wanted to share the revelation I had had during that year with everything that had happened. Jocelyn had brought me courage and simply inspired me to be better. I was hopeful to pass along that message so others, too, would be inspired and be brave about something in their personal lives. Yes, the evening was about raising money to cure Rett Syndrome. But this year I began to see a much bigger picture. A purpose behind everything we were enduring. I did my best in a 15 minute speech, to portray this. According to Dennis, "I nailed it." Making Dennis proud was icing on the cake for the evening.

On the way home, Dennis and I both sighed with relief that another year was over and told each other we did great. We did the "Did you talk to so and so?" Just like we did the night we were married, wanting to make sure all of our guests felt important.

"What do you think this year's total will be?" he asked as we continued to reflect on the evening.

When he asked I fell silent and my thoughts drifted into the Andy Andrews leadership book I was currently reading: "Your words create your world. Speak it into existence."

"$60,000" I finally said with pure confidence.

Dennis chuckled, "Elizabeth, we only brought in $49,000 last year. What did we walk into the evening with, just sponsors and ticket sales?"

"I don't know," I admitted with confidence.

"So why would you think $60,000?"

"I just do" was my only reply. The butterflies in my stomach were doing back flips. Oh how I hoped I was right! I was excited, but not anxious. I knew God had it all in His hands and it would work out the way He intended.

The next morning my mom called. She was done adding up all the sales, donations and auction totals, and gave me an evening total. "Beth, you're not going to believe this! We're over $58,000!"

When I hung up the phone I ran in the other room to tell Dennis

"We're at $58,000!" His mouth dropped and eyes were huge. "Speak it into existence" I explained to him. We did it! By the end of the year with random donations still running in, we made just over $66,000 for RSRT. *Thank you, God! Awesome job!*

I finally arrived to my hotel in Texas. It was a beautiful hotel. Fancy. Marble tile floor, chandeliers for days, a steak house off the lobby entrance. My first thought, *I wish Dennis were here with me.* But I knew, deep down, it just wasn't for him. I won a leadership trip from California to Texas from AdvoCare. Everything in the physical world told me I shouldn't go, but something deeper called me onto the 12 hour, 2 plane switch and 3 hour delay to Arlington, Texas.

I texted my friend, Sharice, telling her that I had finally arrived. As I pulled my luggage on wheels, my anticubital portion of my arms throbbed under my sweater. I was trying to hide the gigantic bruise which left me looking like an IV drug user. The marking was a reminder of what I had just gone through the last 72 hours. Sudden abdominal pain 72 hours ago landed me in a local emergency room. After, I was transferred to a hospital an hour away for further evaluation.

"Gallbladder irritation" and "dehydration from viral infection" was the deciding outcome from my hospitalization. I was discharged from the hospital just 16 hours before I boarded my plane to Texas. Dennis was infuriated with me, to say the least! He was a worried husband and wanted his wife home. I completely understood his feelings. However, I felt I was destined to go on this trip. It was more than just vitamins and AdvoCare. I had to go! And I felt like whatever my body was fighting the week prior was an evil force's desperate attempt to keep me off that plane. But I was stubborn, I was going! There was no compromise, I just didn't know how to explain that rationalization or feeling to my husband.

I empathized with my husband, but boarded the plane regardless. I knew something big laid ahead.

I sat in the lobby waiting for Sharice. I was snacking on saltine crackers when I noticed a quiet man in the corner chewing on a toothpick and gazing at me. Studying me. It didn't make me uncomfortable, just curious. He saw me notice him.

"Are you tired?" he asked out of the blue.

"A little" I answered politely. I didn't know him, but the hotel lobby was crawling with familiar AdvoCare faces. I figured he was friends with one of them.

"You have bricks you've built all around you. God is tearing them down one by one and is rebuilding your life," he blurted out without invitation or worry of what I may say in return. I looked around the room trying to see if anyone was paying attention. *How could he know about my self isolation with Jocelyn a few years ago?* I didn't have a chance to reply, he simply continued,

> "The last two years you haven't been who God created you to be. He is rebuilding your life brick by brick. You've been hurt. You've called out to God in one liners. One liner prayers. I can see them scroll across your forehead. God sees you and hears you. He says, 'Daughter, I see you, I am with you. I know your pain. Trust me, press into me.'"

Tears began falling like rain down my face. By this time, the rest of the room was quiet and listening. Familiar faces in the room who knew about Jocelyn and our journey the past few years also began to cry. I suddenly felt embarrassed about the "one-liner prayers" this stranger was referring to. The shoe day, when I doubted God and cursed him for giving me more than I could handle. My embarrassment quickly subsided as he continued.

"You've had a hard childhood and something about your childhood has recently resurfaced. Don't worry, I am working on your family. Your husband has stress and worries about trying to provide. He feels like a failure. He doesn't sleep. He tosses and turns at night in worry. He will be healed soon and see everything."

As he spoke, I felt down to my left ring finger and felt the absence of my wedding ring, which I took off already in the cab on the way to the hotel, trying to expedite getting ready for bed. My wedding ring was in my carryon! *How did this stranger even know I was married?*

But something punched me in the stomach and I knew this stranger was speaking truth! Dennis did worry and didn't sleep at night because of it. I knew he didn't sleep because I physically felt him toss and turn and he would always tell me how he didn't sleep well. I started realizing, everything this man was telling me was from God, himself.

"It is time for breakthrough," he continued. "For healing beyond your expectations. You are going to dream and I need you to write it down. Write a book. Don't worry about the critics. Don't deny or hide the testimony I have given you. It is for God's glory. What the enemy has intended for bad, will be used to bless others. There will be healing beyond your expectations. He is rebuilding everything, worry not and be ready!"

In 2014, I attended my first "Women of Faith" event. I was so inspired by all of the women who spoke at this event- full of faith but admittedly, a hot mess one time or another during their lives. I was drawn to such honesty and truth. Passionate women, on fire for God, but still sinners and not deserving of God's love. But thank GOD for Jesus who paid for our sins so we are given mercy and grace. These women were speaking my language and I soaked up every word.

Something that stuck with me that weekend, something that God wanted me to hear, was that when we are weak, we rely on Him for strength and then God gets the glory for it, not us. That hit home. I knew God was helping me through so much, but I rarely pointed to Him, to show others, that it was God's doing, not mine. A big lesson learned- give credit where credit is due! I was just taking all the blessings and favor that God was giving and never showing others that God was responsible for it all. How selfish of me! But I wasn't going to beat myself with guilt over it- I was going to change some things.

Then, one of the speakers really got me thinking… soul searching.

She was empowering everyone to do something that scares them, that way, God will show up and help. So, I sat in the audience and tried to figure out what scared me… I decided that I was still worried about what others thought. Fear of rejection, judgment. So if fear is an evil tactic to paralyze me and prevent me from doing God's work, I should be running at my fears, not away from them. *But I already do public speaking once a year,* I argued in my head *that's running at my fears… but maybe that wasn't so scary anymore. Every year got easier…* I was trying to figure out what scared me, what was my purpose. What was my weakness so God could show up and work through me, then get the glory.

Out of all of the speakers and music, somewhere I felt the calling to write a book! I felt it was absolutely ridiculous, but there was no denying what I was feeling! The thought made me sweat, that's how I knew I was on the right path- it scared me! I'm horrible at grammar and spelling. When the ER went to computer charting, the staff was excited for ME because my handwriting is horrible- always has been. I always tell people I write like a chicken and the resemblance really is phenomenal. So grammar, spelling, English in general… NOT my strength.

My thoughts then turned to the Texas hotel lobby 4 months prior, when the stranger was telling me that God wanted me to "Write it down. Write a book. Don't worry about the critics." *Is this for real?* I thought in the middle of the stadium.

The revelation danced in my head for a few days. I had to get it out, let someone know, bounce thoughts off of someone I trusted. I went to Pastor Vinnie: "I think God wants me to write a book… but that's ridiculous! I wouldn't even know where to begin."

He was so kind, "Well, Beth. You have a story to tell, obviously. Just go home and start journaling. See what happens." I was shocked that he wasn't laughing WITH me at the whole ordeal. I was also surprised he thought I had a story. Doubt was still in me, but I did what he advised. I went home and began to write…

*Reachable*

Year four of Jocelyn's Journey was an exciting one. I felt like I was finally committed to Jocelyn's Journey, whereas the first three years I had one foot out the back door. I was willing to do it, "one more time", "one more time"… But year four, during our first committee meeting in January, I shared with the committee a vision. A commitment to Jocelyn's Journey, to continue with the event, even after Rett Syndrome was cured. As I explained to them:

"What would we be teaching our children, if we get what we want, a cure for Rett syndrome, then we all chest bump and go about our lives. There are so many other people out there in need of help. Two people over the past few months have contacted me asking for help or guidance with fundraising. One person's child had cancer, the other, her best friend, was diagnosed with breast cancer. We have learned so much over the years, we can continue with "Jocelyn's Journey" and continue to help others. I don't know exactly how, or what it all entails, I'm just in this for the long haul and I wanted to invite you all to be with me."

Every single committee member voted, "YES!" I was honored to be committed to them and to the event we all had created together, which we all agreed to make bigger and better every year. I was nauseated and thrilled all at once. I decided that I just might be an adrenaline junkie!

We began planning with a goal of $70,000. That would be $10,000 more than the previous year. This also contributed to my nausea, but we all felt that we had to stretch for bigger and we needed a goal. My fear was that it was year four; would people return to our event, what could I do to make it different, more entertaining, more impressive. Honestly, I was worried about keeping people's interest in helping us.    I felt the need to show our supporters, how much we appreciated them. It was always my fear, every year, that I would forget to thank someone. So the theme for the entire year was to be grateful! To put the focus on the committee, guests and all our supporters. To honor them, thank them, put focus on them. We had a "Thank You" goodie bag for each of our guests on the table when they arrived. Inside were several coupons to local businesses (i.e. free ice cream) as well as some small samples from a few of our supporting businesses (brittle, Scentsy bar, and Spark).

We had something special and different for our guests for the presentation piece as well! We met another Rett family through the years, the Miyata's, who have a Rett daughter, Lani, who is now 30 years old. I have always admired this family and their positiveness and love for everyone. I could not imagine what it was like having a Rett girl, 30 years ago, before there was even a blood test for Rett Syndrome to confirm diagnosis. Regardless of the struggles they must have endured, this family was incredible. Lani's sister, Nanea, was extremely talented at producing independent films. She was happy to help us make a very professional 7 minute video to show at our event. You could really tell the difference between her professional video and my little home made videos. We were so grateful for her using her talents to help our event look top notch!

Next, we had a researcher located in Southern California, who RSRT was funding for treatment projects for Rett Syndrome. He did a quick presentation on his project, which RSRT was funding and how it could help our girls. It had a lot to do with diet and the imbalance of natural bacteria in the lining of the gut causing some of the symptoms of Rett Syndrome. It was pretty fascinating and I kept thinking of AdvoCare's probiotics Jocelyn was taking. Coincidence? I think not! It was a total God thing that this researcher, in our back yard, was focusing on nutrition. Pretty incredible. More importantly, however, I was excited that our guests were able to see first hand, what their donations and money were going towards. It was awesome to have him there.

And last, but definitely not least, we had a representative from RSRT in the room for the first time. All the way from New Jersey, RSRT's Program Director, Tim Freeman spoke at our event. Tim was also a Rett parent and he got to share his story with our guests as well as the latest and greatest things going on with RSRT. It was great to have him there, to personally thank our guests for their continued support. I really think our guests appreciated it as well!

While Tim was great at the event, I enjoyed the one on one time we had to chat about our girls and how similar they were. His daughter, Eleanor, was a little over a year younger than Jocelyn. It's always nice to compare notes and see what was working or not working for another Rett girl. Another topic I thoroughly enjoyed picking Tim's brain about was RSRT. "What's going on? How close are we? What's in the mix? How can we help?" Poor Tim got hit with a million questions by the committee. His answers were the same as Monica's, when I asked her my million questions. It was nice for the committee to get it straight from the horses mouth though. I just sat back and listened.

The committee and myself were pleased with the event and how smoothly it ran. Every year we were getting better, and once again, we broke our goal. The evening raised over $72,000!

Something that Tim said during his visit, however, intrigued me. "Beth, if there were ten more families out there that would host an event like Jocelyn's Journey, it would change Rett research." Several emotions flooded in. First, I was honored that he thought our event was so great. Second, I got mad! Mad that something was standing in the way of our girls getting their cure- MONEY. Then my anger turned into excitement. There was something obtainable in the way of changing Rett research. Something was in the way of expediting Jocelyn's cure. I was tired of seeing our girls suffering in the Rett Facebook group. It was time to rise up, and get some money to stop all the suffering and nonsense from this horrible disease! I was absolutely inspired, but I had no idea where to start! *Next year*, I told myself, *Next year's Jocelyn's Journey has to be big! We are close! Close to our goal and the cure!*

## Healing Beyond Expectations

Scoliosis is common with Rett girls and I remember when she got her first brace at 3 years old, I was a mess. I explained to my friend Crystal, "I feel like I just received a death sentence for my daughter." A little dramatic, I admit, but it was when I was living in fear, not faith. I knew that the back brace was to buy time until she had spinal surgery. It was explained to me, at the time, that she couldn't have spinal surgery until she had reached puberty; when her torso was done growing. Fusing the spine, in order to straighten it, would cause her torso to stop growing, but her organs would continue to grow. This could potentially cause heart and lung disease. So, the lesser of two evils, Jocelyn will have scoliosis and this back brace until puberty, then surgery. To be most effective, the brace was supposed to be worn 23 hours, 45 minutes a day. I told the doctor from day one, I would NOT do that to my daughter. She would not be sleeping with it on and it goes so low that it needs to be taken off to go potty. Potty breaks were quiet an ordeal, and could take up to 15 minutes for one trip! The doctors understood and still felt it would be beneficial for Jocelyn to be in a brace.

The back brace may have straightened her a bit, but it was no picnic. It squeezed her so tight that she could not take a deep breath. The doctor reassured me that she could breathe. But I could tell it was difficult for Jocelyn to breath with it on. Rett girls are also at high risk for pneumonia, and not giving Jocelyn her full lung capacity to take a deep breath increased this risk. It was easy to be concerned about it. *I trust she will be okay, I trust she will be okay* I'd pray when my thoughts would drift to worrying about pneumonia. But it wasn't just her little lungs I worried about, it was her gut too! Her brace wraps around her entire torso like an exoskeleton. There is a cut out for her g-tube, with the idea that I could tube feed her with it on. We did so in the beginning. But at the end of her Kindergarden year, Jocelyn began to throw up after every feed. You don't have to be a physicist to see how this makes sense; too much pressure and she explodes! This was unfortunate because it blew Jocelyn's nissen fundoplication (internal sutures preventing Jocelyn from "spitting up" or throwing up). Not having a nissen any longer forced us to stop tube feeds during the night. If she were to throw up during the night, she could aspirate (fluid could go into her lungs) and essentially, she could drown. Again, there is enough to worry about around here to drive a mother bonkers. I gave this whole situation to God and prayed for direction when a change was needed. The entire thing was a mess that only He could fix!

In July of 2015, I was, once again driving down the 101. My thoughts were racing much faster than the LA traffic. The words of Jocelyn's orthopedist who we just saw repeatedly rang through my brain: *Your daughter needs surgery by Christmas!* His mater-of-fact statement repeated in my head as I rubbed my large belly and did a little math. *Jones baby #3 would be around 3 months old at Christmas. What are we going to do?!*

When we got home, Dennis was supervising the swimming pool we were putting in. We had always wanted a pool but we finally pulled the trigger when we decided to build it for aqua therapy for Jocelyn. It was obvious that her spine was curving more and more each week. We thought we were outsmarting the progression of the curve by taking gravity away and putting Jocelyn in water. We even designed the pool ourselves for therapy for Jo. I broke the news to Dennis as he stood over a freshly dug out seven foot hole in our back yard.

"When?" he asked quietly.

"He said maybe around Christmas. We go back in November to discuss pre-op stuff. Her curve is 64 degrees compared to 47 degrees last summer."

"That sucks," Dennis said quietly with a sigh. He picked up a shovel and continued to work on the dirt around our hole. We were finally talking about our daughter having surgery, treatments, and both admitting that Rett was taking a tole on her. We weren't fighting. I wasn't nervous nor did I feel like I was coming up with a random request for spinal surgery. We were talking. We had come a long way from the screaming at each other, unaware of the hypothetical unicorns running down the street the night before her MRI. Or the throwing of spatulas into a hot barbecue when I told Dennis I thought it was time for a g-tube. Bitter sweet, you could say.

That October was our 5th Jocelyn's Journey Gala. It was a challenging year, having 6 week old Abigail Rae to care for, but she did pretty well. And I could feel how strong the committee was. Every year we get bigger, stronger, and better and that was definitely noticed. They managed mostly everything while I made a video and said a speech. In my speech, I announced that Jocelyn would be having spinal surgery within the next six months. I got it out in the open, in a large group setting so I didn't have to explain things one on one with everyone who loved Jocelyn. That was exhausting for me to even think about. It felt good to announce it and get it out in the open.

The highlight of our evening was our guest speaker, Ms. Gaby. A woman in her 20's with Rett Syndrome! She is extremely high functioning with Rett, in that she can walk, use her hands, and type. Gaby wrote a beautiful speech for our event and sat in front of our guests as a computer read it out loud. It was incredible, to hear first hand what it is like to have Rett Syndrome. Though high functioning, Gaby was very anxious about getting in front of a crowd. She said in her speech that she feels like she has to do what she can. To be a voice for the Rett girls who cannot speak up. Incredibly inspiring! The wonderful evening raised over $90,000! Our biggest year yet!

November came and Dennis got the day off to meet with the orthopedic doctor regarding surgery. I came with a list of questions. Probably the usual questions, any parent would have if they went through surgery for their child: "What's recovery time?", "How long will she be in the hospital?", "What pain medicine will she be on and for how long?"… But when I came to some questions, specific to Jocelyn, my stomach turned.

"With this particular surgery, what kind of limitations would a healthy person have? A person without Rett Syndrome?"

"That isn't something we really need to get into," the orthopedist hurried through the question and sat as if in anticipation of my next question so he could get on with his day.

"Well, I just want to make sure I am not limiting her on having a normal life after she is cured of Rett Syndrome. Will she be able to do dance, cheerleading, have children…?" I explained myself, wanting an answer.

"There won't be a cure for your daughter."

Silence fell over the room. An uncomfortable silence and I could feel my face turning red. Dennis re-adjusted in his chair as he knew things were about to get uncomfortable.

"There may be a way to prevent Rett Syndrome one day, but there won't be a cure for her," the orthopedist could sense my rage through my silence. He knew I was highly offended. It wasn't so much that he crushed my beliefs, as if he just told me there was no Santa Clause. It was that he had no clue what Rett Syndrome was. For years we had been coming to this doctor and we liked him, trusted him. He claimed to have many patients with Rett Syndrome. So why in the world didn't he understand or know what causes Rett Syndrome- which is absolutely nothing! It happens at random! And to act educated on the subject and tell me there may be a way to prevent it one day… *How in the world would that be possible?! Symptoms are typically not prevalent until age 2!* My trust with this doctor went flying out the window. And as a human, my respect for him was fading as quickly as my face was turning red. *Who talks to a parent like this?! Especially about something they obviously know nothing about!*

"Do you have any more questions for me?" he interrupted my tantrum in my head. I shuffled through my papers to find my place again.

"Yes," I was able to whisper out. "When we first came to you when Jocelyn was 3 years old, you said that we had to wait for surgery until her torso was done growing, which probably wouldn't be until puberty. Otherwise she may end up with lung and heart problems. She's only 7 years old. Aren't we worried about creating problems later in life with this surgery?"

The man smiled, sympathetically at me. Somehow he looked smaller in his little chair than when we first entered the room. He held his hand up towards the direction of my mouth, shook his head back and forth while softly speaking, "She needs this surgery. This is the one she needs." He stood up and headed to the door. "The surgery staff will call you in a few weeks to schedule the surgery date," and he walked out.

I sat for a minute in disbelief. I was hit by yet another train in a doctors office. I was trying to make sense of what had just happened as Dennis was working around me gathering our things and our 3 children, "Let's go," he snapped me out of my paralyzing stare. I got up and followed Dennis out.

Not a word. I didn't speak a word. I had no tears either. I was just sick with this doctor, his bedside manner, his indirect answers to my questions… the mixed emotions left me confused on how to react. *Do I cry in helplessness? Do I yell in anger? Do I fight? But who do I fight?* It wasn't until we were half way home when we stopped for lunch that my silence broke.

"Are you going to say ANYTHING, Elizabeth?" Dennis asked concerned. He'd never seen me so silent, and honestly, I'd never been. I was mentally digesting. I couldn't even pray. I was just on replay.

"Did he just say 'There won't be a cure for your daughter, but maybe a way to prevent Rett Syndrome one day'?" was all I could mutter out. I felt like I was in a dream, or a nightmare rather. I needed confirmation that that really just happened.

"Yes, Beth. But he isn't an expert in Rett Syndrome. He's an orthopedic surgeon, let him be an expert in that," my husband tried to comfort me. Back into my silence I went. I felt lost. Helpless. My daughter was at the mercy of this man, who didn't believe in her. I felt stupid for liking and trusting him for all of these years, and now suddenly, I couldn't stand to be in the same room with him.

*No cure?! NO CURE!* I screamed in my head while appearing silent to the world during our lunch. *I sweat blood and tears for Jocelyn's Journey, for our cure. The entire committee dedicates so much time to us, for Jocelyn's cure. And this man is so confident that its all for nothing?!*

Then my thoughts traveled to the first day I met this doctor. When we decided to brace her. My dramatic text to Crystal Gax, "I feel like I just received a death sentence for my daughter." It suddenly seemed that that text, that feeling, was pointing to this moment. Helpless and defeated, I stayed in silence for days.

A week after our appointment, I happened to be on Facebook when

I saw a picture on one of my Rett Syndrome support group pages. It was a before and after of an 8 year old Rett girl with a 64 degree curve pre-op and a 0 degree curve post-op. It was an incredible sight. I was intrigued with how straight her surgeon got the spine. Our orthopedist told us he could only straighten it by 50%. I messaged the mom right away and asked for details on her daughter and her surgery. The mom used the term "growing rods". *AMAZING!* These "growing rods" allow a young scoliosis spine to continue to grow post op, so that the patient wouldn't develop lung and heart problems in the future! *Incredible! I wasn't dreaming when our orthopedist told me that when Jocelyn was 3!*

Hope quickly fueled me and I began to do my homework. I found a doctor in Los Angeles who did these "growing rods". He actually designed a lot of the hardware he used himself. I contacted our insurance and asked to be sent there for a second opinion. I was informed that only the first opinion physician could order a second opinion referral. So I e-mailed him immediately. Even typing to him a conversation made me feel ill. I just knew that he wasn't the right doctor for us anymore. He replied a few days later:

"Mrs. Jones, I also do growing rods and I will not be doing them on your daughter as she is not a candidate. I feel that any other second opinion would agree with me on the matter so I will not be sending you to the requested second opinion, outside of our network. Feel free to make an appointment to talk about this further."

*Done! I am done!* In my opinion, any doctor that isn't more than happy to send a patient to get a second opinion is prideful and cannot be trusted! Not to mention, I knew that it was not legal to refuse a second opinion, outside of an insurance network. But I didn't have time to go the legal route, that could take years! Jocelyn's back was getting worse by the week and I needed to act NOW to get her what she needed. I had no idea where to start, but I had a goal: growing rods and the amazing doctor in Los Angeles.

*Thank God I was on Facebook that night and saw that post.* I prayed and prayed for direction, discernment and for alignment with people who would help me. I got on the phone, I kept a list. When someone said "call back Monday," I did so at 9am, right when the older girls went to school. In my bathrobe and pajamas, trying to tend to my newborn, I was on the phone, sending faxes, e-mails, signing things… you name it. It reminded me so much of movies where parents are on the phone, fighting for their sick kids. Yep, that was me! For months! Before I dialed a phone number or put a letter in the mailbox, I prayed. I started my quest in November and, by the grace of God, we got an appointment to see the amazing doctor in Los Angeles at the end of March.

I was grateful Dennis had the day off and was coming with me to the new "amazing" orthopedist. I was nervous. A bit scared that he would, in fact, agree with the first orthopedist that Jocelyn wouldn't be a candidate for growing rods. Regardless, I had to try! She deserved the chance to have healthy lungs and a heart! When I got nervous, I thought of a future scenario of Jocelyn being 20 years old, cured of Rett but suffering from heart and lung problems because I didn't question the first ortho doctor. Knowing what I discovered, I just had to try! And there we were, in the office of the man I trusted with my daughter's spine more than anyone, and I hadn't even met him yet!

Dr. Amazing came in and greeted us and Jocelyn and each of her sisters with a kind, genuine smile. He explained that his x-ray that day showed that Jocelyn's spine was now at 72 degrees and that she does, in fact, need surgery. He suggested a rod he designed which would straighten her spine and allow her torso to continue to grow, however he didn't call them growing rods. They had a fancy name, probably because he had patented it. *Call it whatever you want, we're in!* We scheduled Jocelyn's surgery that day for April 20- just 3 weeks away.

The week before surgery day, we were completely honest with our girls, especially Jocelyn. We told her she needed surgery to fix her back and make her sit up straight again, and that she wouldn't need a brace ever again. We told her it was going to hurt and that she would be in the hospital for a few days, maybe a week. We explained that she could not return to school until after the summer, so she could get better and stronger at home. Any time we talked about it with Jo, she smiled. She sometimes giggled. Even the night before surgery, Dennis Jocelyn and I went to dinner in Los Angeles and we explained again, that we were fixing her back, it was going to hurt and that we were with her and wouldn't leave her side once it was over. She smiled and giggled. Dennis and I were confused as to whether she understood. She always seemed to understand most things that we would talk to her about, even though she couldn't reply verbally. Then it struck me, *Maybe she's happy to get her back straight because it already hurts.* Whatever the case may be, she was a trooper and went with the flow, just as she usually does.

The morning of, Jocelyn was in good spirits and didn't complain at all. I worried, as I usually did on a procedure day, that she would be starving. But Jo was absolutely fine. We wore our Jocelyn's Journey t-shirts and posted a picture of the three of us on social media. We had asked our followers and supporters to also wear their Jocelyn's Journey gear and post a picture of it so I could show Jocelyn, once she woke up, how many people were thinking and praying for her. Setting all of that up kept me busy in the waiting room, until we were called back to get her ready for surgery.

In pre-op, Jocelyn got into a gown, was put on a monitor and had her IV placed. This was it, we were a go. Dr. Amazing walked in and kindly greeted all three of us, then he got serious:

"So, I was thinking about Jocelyn all weekend and I think the best technique to do, that will straighten the spine the most, is to place a few screws into her head and apply gentle traction while we work on her spine."

*A halo?* My medical mind began to race as my head seem to involuntarily nod in agreement. In my peripheral vision, I could see Dennis also nodding. *It makes sense, but I'm not ready for this! I was worried about her spine. Now her skull is being drilled into too as well? Her precious, tiny, skull?!*

Dr. Amazing continued, "So the nurse will bring in a form for you to sign agreeing to this. But also, Rett patients typically have trouble with nutrition after such an invasive surgery. If there's ever a complication, typically it has to do with the gut. So, we'd like to put in a large IV in her arm, that will last a long time and can handle IV fluid that is 100% nutrition. It's called TPN."

*Dr. Dudrick, the AdvoCare doctor who invented TPN, crosses my path yet again.* My tired, wandering brain returned to the conversation. As a nurse, I understood the rationale for the central line for the possible need for TPN, but as a mom, I wasn't prepared. *A halo... A PICC (peripherally inverted central catheter)?!*

"Okay," Dennis and I both agreed without consulting with each other. It was a lot to take in all at once. But then I reminded myself that I had prayed for this doctor, for this team. I prayed that God put us wherever He wanted us to be and that I would trust Him. So there we were, and there we went, signing more consents.

During the pre-op doctor visit, the nurse was giving Jocelyn sleepy medication. She looked drunk- a look Dennis and I were familiar with on her before other procedures. But it still made us giggle. A bit of a distraction to all the seriousness we were discussing.

About ten minutes after the doctor left, a team of operating room staff came in to take Jocelyn in. I stayed calm. They began to wheel her bed down a hallway. Still calm. Then the redline painted on the ground came. The forbidden red line. One of the nurses turned to me and told me to give her a kiss and empathetically reassured me, "We've got her mom. It's okay, we will call you shortly."

"Okay, thank you," I muttered out very loudly. "I'll see you in a minute Sissy. I love you." Then giant snot bubbles with crocodile tears suddenly appeared on my face and I was ugly crying at the red line.

My husband took me in his arms and attempted to comfort me. "Hey, hey, hey…" he calmly whispered as I choked and cried. We were taken to a little office room where I could collect myself. By the time I could see again, I looked up at Dennis and his eyes were swollen and red as well. I cleaned up my face, collected myself as best as I could, then we went to the main waiting area.

After about an hour of being away from our first born, we finally got a call. The sweet voice identified herself as one of the OR nurses and she explained, "It took a while to set up, but we are just now getting started."

"Okay, thank you so much, please keep us informed. I really appreciate it," I replied professionally.

Dennis and I did our usual waiting dance. We ate, played some cards, I colored, then we both were playing on our phones. I checked social media and was suddenly uplifted. The outpour of support from our family and friends posting pictures of themselves wearing Jocelyn's Journey gear was absolutely breathtaking. I started to cry again. Make up that day was absolutely pointless. So many people showing love helped me sit in that waiting room for over 4 hours. And then, Dr. Amazing walked in the room. Dennis and I eagerly stood up to greet him.

"Everything went well," he explained. "I got her spine to be straighter than I anticipated so I'm glad we used the traction. She is being sewn up right now, then they will take her to her room to be recovered for about an hour. Someone will call you when you can see her. Do you have any questions?" Dr. Amazing seemed even more amazing when he told us this news. I cried again. Dennis thanked him and we both sighed with relief as we sat back down.

*Hurdle one over,* I told myself. *Now lets get her recovered!* I was eager to see her, see her face. I wanted to make sure she wasn't hurting. I also wanted her to know we were there, with her and she wasn't alone.

About an hour went by and we asked a nice lady at the desk in the waiting room if we could go see her. She called the ICU and we got the green light. I started to eagerly question the desk lady as if she had answers:

"Is she intubated? Is she in pain? Is she awake?" I continued as Dennis answered for the nice lady.

"Come on, Elizabeth." I followed his lead and up the elevators we went.

But when we reached her room, there was a team of doctors, nurses, therapists in there for my tiny daughter. At first glance I was worried with all the attention she was receiving. Through the crowd, I strived to peek in and catch a glimpse of her. Finally, a portable X-ray machine moved out of the way and I could see my sweet girl laying in bed. She wasn't even on oxygen. I looked at the monitor and her oxygen level was 98%. My girl was doing incredible! Off the ventilator, not needing oxygen and just sleeping peacefully so she wasn't in pain. I suddenly felt like I could breath!

We stood out of everyone's way as much as we could. The staff was incredible and inviting. Some asked questions about her baseline, or what her activities were on a normal day. Others asked about her medical history, just to confirm with what they already had in the chart. My favorite though was when someone commented on how well she was doing and how well she looked. It made my heart dance. I was so hopeful that the hard part was over.

As things calmed down, Jocelyn's ICU nurse and I began to talk. She was sweet and shared her experiences as an RN. I admitted I didn't think I could ever work in pediatrics, and especially not pediatrics ICU. I explained that I would just be sad at the bad outcomes and may not be able to handle it. I shared with her some of my experiences as an ER nurse and she admitted she never wanted to do ER. We both chuckled and were enjoying our conversation. It felt good- I felt like a nurse and not a patient's mom for a minute. But then reality set back in as she changed the subject:

"Are you the type of mom who wants to know everything? Even the scary stuff or would you just rather not know?"

"I'm the type of mom who wants to know everything," I admitted as I suddenly became concerned with this odd question. "Well, Jocelyn developed prolonged QT interval right after anesthesia. They pulled ismolol and put pacer pads on her. There was a delay getting started with the actual surgery because of it, but it started to normalize and they were able to perform the surgery. She did really well the remaining surgery and they didn't have to give her any medications. I would just want to know that if I were her mother so I wanted you to know. Maybe ask the doctors about it when they do rounds again."

"Okay, thank you for telling me, I really appreciate it," I replied softly, trying to take in what she had said. So, in layman terms, Jo's heart went into a funny rhythm, called prolonged QT interval. This electrical abnormality can be dangerous because it can be a pre-cursor to torsades de pointe, or polymorphic tachycardia- which are pulseless rhythms. Where "shocking" or defibrillating is needed to restart the heart, hoping it goes into a normal rhythm. To put plainly, there was a risk that Jocelyn could have coded.

Later that evening as I was watching Jocelyn's heart monitor every second, I began to daydream about my text to Crystal Gax when Jocelyn was first diagnosed with scoliosis, "I feel like I just got a death sentence for my daughter." *Did I know, back then. Why did I think that back then? People live with scoliosis all the time. And now, I just learned, she very easily could have coded.* My thoughts turned to my fight to get to Dr. Amazing and to this facility. I was suddenly grateful for the entire ordeal. *Thank you GOD for that mean first orthopedic doctor which lead to the devine chain of events and brought us here, right where we are supposed to be.*

Jocelyn's surgery was on a Wednesday and we were able to take her home on Sunday. She was doing incredible! Better than I would have been. I was so happy to take her home, but I was dreading the 2 hour ride home. We medicated her and buckled down and made it home with Jocelyn complaining only the last 15 minutes. It was the longest she had been out of bed since surgery. But we made it, and we were finally home! My baby was in her own bed! It was incredible! The next 3 days I spent with Jocelyn in her bed, and getting her up in a wheelchair 1-2 times a day, trying to increase the time each day, as the physical therapist in the hospital instructed us. Things were going smoothly.

Day 4 of being home, however, we had to return to Los Angeles for a wound check. I was nervous about the long car ride there and back, all in one day. It was only 8 days after her surgery. Dennis and I packed up and headed out early with Jocelyn and Baby Abigail. We sent Rylee to school because we figured it would be a boring day for her, and a bit stressful for us having all three girls.

The doctors were pleased with the healing of her incision and her overall recovery. One doctor mentioned that Jocelyn had the shortest hospital stay after spinal surgery for a Rett girl. She reiterated that they typically have trouble with feedings and nutrition. I explained that we did too in the hospital, when the doctors wanted to give her formula first, versus the home blends I do with mostly AdvoCare products. *Thank God for AdvoCare!* I silently praised. *We could have still been in the hospital right now!* I recalled two episodes of Jocelyn vomiting "coffee ground" stomach contents when formula was being given, which indicates blood in the stomach. Finally, our last night in the hospital, my little 7 year old's tummy was rounded and firm. Her gut was getting swollen. I got out my mama bear voice and refused any more feedings through her g-tube. "Her gut needs rest," I explained myself. The staff obliged and the next morning I was allowed to do our usual feeds. Her tummy flattened, she seemed more comfortable, and we went home that afternoon. *I know my girl!*

On the way home from the appointment, I was grateful there was no Los Angeles traffic. We stopped to get gas and it made me a bit anxious. "Dennis, hurry please. Jo is getting uncomfortable. This is the longest she's been out of bed. She really needs to lay down."

"Yes, Elizabeth. It will take even longer to get home if we run out of gas," he replied. I understood, I just hurt for my girl and she was beginning to complain a bit, despite the medications I gave before we left the hospital. I wanted to be home, in her bed, watching a movie on her TV that Santa conveniently brought her this past Christmas. She loved her hair pet and snuggles and someone just to talk to her. I couldn't do that while she was in the back seat.

Finally we were back on the road. *Okay, almost done. We don't have another appointment for at least 3 weeks.* I was still homesick from being in the hospital for 5 days. Then I turned my anxiety into gratitude. The near misses we escaped with the prolonged QT interval, the blood in her stomach with her rounded tummy, and not to mention how straight her spine is and just a successful surgery. *Thank you God!*

Texas suddenly came to mind. *Maybe this was the "healing beyond expectations" he was referring to.* Despite my gratefulness, I was hopeful it wasn't it. I wanted her cured and in the Olympics winning a gold metal at something. That would be beyond my expectations. I chuckled out to myself as I watched a white car a short distance away get pushed into our lane:

**WHAM!**

It was the loudest silence I had ever heard. We were moving, then we were all completely still. I realized, I couldn't breath. *This is it. Oh my goodness! I'm about to meet Jesus. Dennis will be fine, he's a great dad. Gax will make sure my children aren't sad and that they'll understand I love them but I'm with Jesus. Here we go, I can't believe it, but here we go.*

Just as I was mentally prepared to go to heaven, I inhaled a tiny breath and pain filled my body. My breathes got bigger and bigger. *Oh, I got the wind knocked out of me,* I finally rationalized. *Smoke, I see smoke! Why aren't the kids crying?!* Panic set in once I realized I wasn't going to die.

"Are you okay?" Dennis was able to finally mutter out.

"Yes, it hurts to breath," I admitted. "Why aren't the kids making noise? There's smoke!" I tried to yell, still trying to breath. I attempted to open my door. Suddenly I could yell, "Dennis! My door is stuck. Get me out of here! Get my kids out of this car NOW! Why is there smoke?!"

"Calm down! I see Jo, she's awake, probably scared," he tried to comfort me as he opened his door. I managed to get my legs over the center console and exited his side. The white car was sitting side by side next to my Tahoe, on Baby Abbie's side.

"Get the baby Dennis! Do you see her?! Is she okay?! Get her out." I noticed there was no smoke outside of the car. *The airbags. The smoke was from all the airbags.* I was finally comforted, but as I saw our entire tank of gas on the road, I panicked again. *I still can't breath normally. I'm hurting everywhere. How am I going to get Jo's wheelchair out of the car?!* We now had an audience from the mobile home park right next to us. Mama lion came out with vengeance and I yelled as best I could while trying to breath, "MY DAUGHTER IS IN A WHEELCHAIR. SHE JUST HAD SPINAL SURGERY. I NEED HER OUT OF THE CAR! I NEED HER WHEELCHAIR." Several young men went to the back of the Tahoe and got out Jocelyn's wheelchair, which was tossed around back there from the impact. *Thank God we sent Rylee to school!* I looked over at Dennis and saw him get Baby Abbie out of the car. I sighed with relief at her "happy someone picked her up" 7 month old smile. Dennis then went around to Jocelyn's door and had to pry it open. All I could see was airbag, then, finally, he got Jocelyn out! She was NOT happy. She was taking short breaths as if about to cry. We laid her down on her wheelchair. I was so relieved to have my family out of the car, awake, no blood to be noted… Still unable to stand up straight I went to Jo and checked her out as best I could.

"Hey Sissy. I'm so sorry, we have to go back to the hospital and take some pictures now. I'll give you some medicine when we get there. It'll be okay," I tried to comfort my frustrated, confused daughter who just wanted to rest.

We were less than a mile away from home, which meant, our friends, at Apple Valley Fire Department, came to our rescue. It was so nice to see a familiar face holding Baby Abbie. (Thanks Jake!) Dennis was trying to collect our things and I sat by Jo as I watched my off duty fireman pry open the passenger door that I couldn't open. I was proud of him, seeing first hand what he did every day at work. I have to admit, I despite my painful breathing, I managed to get flirty butterflies watching my husband. And then I realized, I was so worried about the kids, I hadn't asked my husband if he was okay. I managed to get up and walk over.

"Babe, are you okay? I'm sorry I haven't asked you yet."

"My hand hurts," as he looked down at swollen knuckles. It wasn't until we noticed the blood on the windshield that we realized the airbag made his hand fly up and break the thick glass.

As the ambulance was loading up Jocelyn and myself, I looked back at my mangled Tahoe. I loved that truck. As soon as Dennis and I found out we were pregnant with Jocelyn, we sold my 2 door Civic and bought the Tahoe. We wanted a bigger, safer family vehicle. She was good to us and gave us a good 9 years.

An Apple Valley Sheriff's Officer came to the back of the ambulance and took down our information. He then exclaimed, "It's a good thing you were in that big SUV, otherwise this would have been a tragic scene right now."

As I nodded my head, tears fell down my cheeks. All I could think was, "healing beyond expectations".

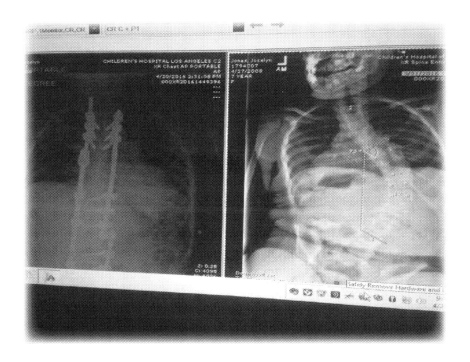

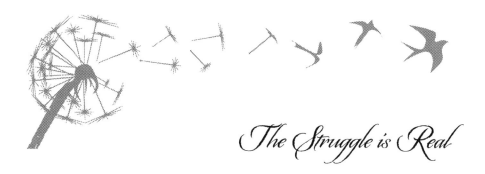

# The Struggle is Real

Living for Jesus is great! Knowing I'm a forgiven sinner is priceless. Having the best advocate to consult with when decisions need to be made is life changing. However, being a Christian does not mean I am perfect or think I am perfect. I am still a sinner in a fallen world. It takes exercise to be faithful to your beliefs. I wouldn't work hard at the gym for a year, get a solid, ripped body and then quit going to the gym. I would have to keep going to the gym to maintain the physique. The same is true for living the life of a Christian. It takes practice, then when you get good at it, you keep practicing!

*The Pride Struggle:*

I've always struggled with pride when it comes to Jocelyn, and I still do. She's never walked, but when she was a toddler, we just got a bigger stroller, a jogging one. Then she looked like every other 2 year old, just catching a ride. It wasn't until she was 3 that we were forced to get her a real wheelchair. To continue to receive therapy when she turned 3, we had to send her to preschool. To get to preschool the school district arranged for a little bus to do curb side pick up. She therefore had to be in an approved wheelchair by the Department of Transportation, which can be anchored down to the bus. I hated that wheelchair for what it represented: a handicap child. It was so definite.

My prideful issues with Jocelyn continued throughout the years. One of the big ones is with her appearance. She tongue flicks and sometimes drools, but I adamantly refuse to put a bib on her. I feel they are distracting from my gorgeous girl. So, I'm therefore picky with her shirts. They have to be dark so no spit or remittances of food can be easily seen. I am completely aware that if she wore a bib, this would eliminate this problem, but I refuse. And the tongue flicking itself is somewhat a pride issue with me. When I remind her to "stop your tongue", she is able to, usually. All day, sometimes, "Stop your tongue! Stop your tongue!..." but she can do it, so I hold her accountable for it. It bothers me because it is, again, distracting when someone is talking to her. AND, it is distracting to HER! When Jo's tongue is having a very active day, it seems that is all she is focusing on. Typically she does it more when something is bothering her: she's tired, a stomach ache, she has to go potty or she's bored. It's just another reminder, right on her face, that the Rett monster is controlling my daughter. And it upsets me. I'm also prideful of her pants. No white on the bottom and nothing too tight on her butt without a long shirt to cover her butt. I don't want people to notice she is wearing a pull up. Jocelyn knows how to go potty on the potty, but has "accidents" because she cannot verbally tell me when she has to go. So, I'm not sure if that's a pride thing or me trying to keep her dignity.

In any case, I admit, I am a sinner and I am prideful! I struggle with this daily and I know I'm not supposed to care what others think. But I just want the world to know that my 8 year old daughter is in there seeing, hearing, and thinking about you looking at her. If I keep her looking as "typical" as possible, I feel people will treat her and talk to her like any other 8 year old. Most people do not take the time to do this, especially if she is tongue flicking like crazy or drooling on herself. At a glance, it would then appear that she isn't aware of her surroundings or the world. But that is not the case.

I also struggle with pride for myself. I've been an "A student" my entire life and have always graduated with honors. I've worked since I was 16. I hold many initials: RN, BSN, PHN, CLNC. And what do I do? Since October 2013, I've been a stay at home mom! Sure I dabble in work from home side jobs, but nothing I'd call an income. In fact, I do it so little that the IRS doesn't even consider it income. It's very hard for me to sit back and watch my husband work so hard at work, while I'm home folding laundry and meal planning. (Yes, I understand I do more than that.) But there are some days, I get into a mopey mood and feel sorry for myself.

I think to myself, *I'm an RN! I could be making money! I'm well educated! I'm well credentialed! I have experience!...* Once my self loathing is over, I remind myself: *I am right where I'm supposed to be. God put me here for a reason. My initials don't matter. The most important title I'd like the world to see on me is "Daughter of God"!* This battle goes on every couple of months. I have to exercise my faith and trust that God will use me where He needs me, when He needs me. Right now, He wants me home with my girls.

This world has also put negative labels that, which, I chose to listen to, could cause some doubt and disbelief: FAILURE, failure to thrive, neurotic nurse, ridiculous, exaggerator, attention seeker, possible Munchausen's, strict, mean, anti-social, bad friend, selfish and "enjoying the attention of being a 'special parent'"". I choose to listen to truth and my most important title: "Daughter of God"! Again, it's an exercise to be able to choose to not listen to negative labels (or lies) this world has placed on me. The struggle is real.

## The Isolation Struggle

One of the biggest lies that I believed for so long was that I was alone. I like to think of this lie as the gateway to sin. When Jocelyn was showing signs of being delayed, I began to feel alone. That was when jealousy, envy, then eventually hate filled my heart. The feeling that I was alone grew stronger and stronger with every sinful emotion that I allowed to enter my world. I soon began to choose to be alone, to isolate myself and my family. It was too painful to see others and it only fed my rage. When I was forced to be around others, I would try and drown my envy in alcohol, which then led to more sin. Dennis and I would then fight. My actions were not honoring my husband at all and the envious hatred in my heart for others cost friendships. The tinniest lie, "I am alone", led to a sin of hatred, which led to more sin.

The truth was, I wasn't alone. We have come so far in our journey through the first year of Jocelyn's life, diagnosis, growing our family and fundraising events... There was no way we could have survived all of that on our own. God was with us, every day, every doctor appointment, every tear, He was with us.

To this day, even though I am not alone, I still struggle with isolation.

Recovering Jocelyn from spinal surgery left us at home, sometimes confined to only her room, for weeks. Then, to top that off, even if I wanted to leave, I had no vehicle because of our accident. Even though I knew it would be for a short period of time, I felt trapped. I do not sit still well. I'm a social person. To be confined to our home for weeks on end, some of my old feelings returned as I watched my friends on social media, out in the world living their life. Envy filled me. Then anger. I recognized my pattern and put it to a stop as quickly as I could and focused on the bigger picture: We were home with Jocelyn, some girls were not so lucky after spinal surgery and spent weeks in the hospital! We all survived a pretty significant car accident. We had food to eat and friends I could call at the drop of a hat that would bring us groceries if we needed them. It took some time, but as I started replacing my envious, angry thoughts with grateful ones, I became happier and more at peace. Isolation is an evil thing! That struggle is very real to so many people, I am sure of it!

## The Parenting Struggle

I know, all of my children belong to God. I gave up fighting with Him for control years ago. However, I sometimes catch myself wanting all of the control again instead of trusting Him and His plan for them. Sometimes this tug of war starts first thing in the morning. I usually wake up at 630am on my own. If I don't hear Jocelyn making her sweet noises from her bed, I fear the worst and panic sets in. On Facebook, I occasionally read about "another Rett girl, losing her battle with Rett", which is usually how it is worded by grieving families. Sudden and unexplained death is a risk for our girls. Some say it is attributed to cardiac issues or breathing problems. It seems to occur sometime during the night. In the morning, parents wake to find their daughter, tucked into bed just as they routinely laid her down the night prior, cold and lifeless under the covers. EVERY morning I wake before Jocelyn, fear sets in that we will be the next "another Rett girl…" on Facebook. Especially with the new complication of an episode of prolonged QT interval. With every step toward her room, I pray and convince myself "Please God, No! Please God, No! Please God, No!" until I creep into her room and see the blankets rise and fall with her breathing. Then I praise, "Thank you, Lord! Thank you, Lord!..." all the way to the shower.

Another struggle for me in trusting God with Jocelyn is when she leaves me and goes to school. I rely on staff, teachers and therapists to not only care for her basic needs, but also on her developmental and educational needs. We've had an awesome staff, who go above and beyond. And we've had a not so awesome staff, who barely interact with Jo. It's frustrating, as a parent, when staff changes not only for the loss of a relationship with them, but the training. Rett Syndrome is rare, so chances are, new staff will have never heard of it, let alone have ever worked with a child with Rett. Training on Rett alone can take weeks. Then there's a whole new training on how Rett effects Jocelyn, specifically.

Then there's the Tobii drama. The Tobii is Jocelyn's communication device. It is basically software on an everyday tablet with an attachment bar on the bottom that contains 5 cameras. The cameras are calibrated to Jocelyn's eyes so she manipulates the tablet by looking at buttons. For staff to become comfortable with using the Tobii, and how to use it for communication with Jocelyn takes months, even years. When there is a turnover with staff at school, it stresses me out! I struggle for it not to, while trying to remain calm and trust that things will work out, but it is definitely an internal struggle for me.

When Jocelyn went from 1st to 2nd grade, Jocelyn's teachers and I decided to change the entire team who was Jocelyn's 1:1 para-educators. I was extremely nervous about the switch, but after praying about it and giving it to God, it actually turned out to be the best decision we've ever made for her school life.

We got assigned Ms. Sara. "Super Sara" I call her. Ms. Sara is a sweet young woman, full of energy and loves Jocelyn. She has great ideas and is always eager to try new things which may help Jocelyn. Ms. Sara has been such a blessing to Jo, her school team, and our family. And, to top it off, she's an LVN so she's not afraid of Jocelyn's medical needs, such as tube feedings. So when I let Go, and let God handle it, it turned out to be better than I could've imagined! We are again in the process of Jocelyn getting an entire new team at school, including her general education teacher, special education teacher, speech therapist, and an awesome administrator at the district who was always so helpful to us. I could easily freak out, not knowing how 3rd grade is going to look for Jocelyn, but I'm grateful we still have Super Sara. And, I'm just letting go and letting God figure it out. Sometimes I get a sense of humor out of it and chuckle to God, "Wow, what a mess! But I know you can handle it!"

There is so much in this world that my children will hear that could create fear, hopelessness, and doubt. It is therefore, my goal to teach them at a young age to default their thought process immediately to truth. For example, the other day, Rylee was explaining that she was scared of monsters. I explained that there are no such things as monsters and she argued with me. So I pointed her to find truth- we got out her bible. That night we read and read and never came across a "monster". I explained that the bible only speaks truth and if the bible doesn't talk about monsters, they don't exist. Rylee's believing heart accepted my explanation and slept great that night.

Because we live in a fallen world and I am a sinner, I understand that I will fail at being a parent. I am not perfect and I show my girls that I know I am not perfect by admitting when I'm wrong and apologizing. There is only one perfect parent, and that is God, the Father. I will do my best to help my children throughout their entire life. However, I will not understand every trial that they go through. So I teach them about someone who will understand every struggle they will face: Jesus. When Jocelyn was in the hospital, recovering from spinal surgery, I had no idea what kind of pain she was experiencing or how she was feeling. But, I told her of someone who did: Jesus! I found a picture of Him on my smart phone and explained to her:

"He had a crown of thorns that were punctured into His head, just like you had screws in your head so the doctor could pull your back straight. He had wounds on His feet, just like you have little sores on your feet from little electrodes they used in surgery [to ensure nerve impulses maintained intact]. His back was scared and bloody, like yours. He had wounds on His hands, just like you have all of these IV's and this one is an arterial line. And finally, He was stabbed in the tummy and it hurt Him, just like your tummy is hurting you right now. Talk to Jesus all about it, girl. He hears your thoughts when you pray to Him. He knows what you are going through, Mommy does not."

## The Marriage Struggle

It is biblical to honor your husbands then your children. Jocelyn is 100% total care, 24/7. It is hard for me to put my husband before her, and he would never ask me to. But I do feel like Dennis gets neglected as I am not the wife I could be, had Jocelyn not had Rett Syndrome.

I remember learning in nursing school that parents with special needs children, a sick child, or a child who has died, have a higher divorce rate than those who don't. I looked at Dennis differently on D-day. I was pregnant, our daughter was just diagnosed with a horrific syndrome and I thought for sure Dennis was going to leave me. Maybe not right away, but eventually. My anxiety that day increased when my thoughts would spin from *How do I help Jocelyn* to *How am I going to be a single mom of two?!* Over the next few weeks, leading into years, I became defensive towards Dennis, knowing this horrible, possible fate. My trust was dwindling by no fault of his own. Always echoing in the back of my head was *probable divorce*. I understood why this statistic may be true. Jocelyn took up so much time and energy from the both of us, not to mention any disputes we had about her care. We strived for date nights but we were very limited on babysitters. Most were intimidated by Jocelyn's needs. There came a point where I could see how divorce would be probable. I never, not for one second, wanted to divorce Dennis! There were days that I just wanted a break. I watched co-workers who were divorced go out for adult time when their kids were "with their dad". They got a break every other weekend. I didn't need that much of a break, just a night or two, every few months would've been incredibly life changing. I also knew Dennis needed a break from the stressful monotony of what our lives had become. I felt bad that I couldn't give him the break he needed or deserved, because I needed one myself. Then, it would turn into a fight over who needed a break more. We were in a downward spiral and we had no clue how to get out!

Over time I realized how dedicated Dennis was to me and his family. Years had passed and he was still devoted. My love for him never changed, and my trust began to come back, what saved us was right in front of our faces on our wedding day. "So they are no longer two but one flesh. What therefore God has joined together, let no man separate" (Matthew

19:6). God brought Dennis and I together, He has been with us through so many troubles and He is still with us today. Why then, would He endure all of that work thus far, only to let us fall apart. No, He wouldn't do that. So I made the decision to stop listening to the LIE of the statistic "probable divorce". Perhaps in numbers, studies and research, one could prove this to be "true". But it is not true for Dennis and I. Our truth comes from God and He says He brought us together and no one can separate. We choose to take no part in this statistic. That does not mean we won't have hard times, but we now endure those hard times, knowing, it will not break us.

## The Perception Struggle

Despite all the struggle the past few years, Dennis and I also had some very exciting times. In 2011, the economy was just right and we were looking to get a bigger home. Our home seemed to be getting smaller with all of the therapy equipment and developmental toys we had accumulated. However, I could not get rid of those toys. I still have them to this day. I am keeping them until Jocelyn is cured. She may still need to develop the fine motor skills of a large puzzle then advance to a peg puzzle, for example. We've invested thousands and I cannot wait to put them to use for Jocelyn, again. So needless to say, we were outgrowing our home. In our quest for a larger home, a must was a split floor plan. I felt bad that Rylee would be far away from me, but not Jocelyn, she needed her space! At night, she needed an entire half of whatever home we purchased. Her "night time parties" were keeping Dennis and I so sleep deprived it was horrible! We desperately needed a split floor plan, and we found one!

We moved into our new home one month after our first Jocelyn's Journey event in 2011. We would joke with our friends on how this would look for an outsider, that we just raised $53,000 then bought a bigger house. And then the joke turned a little serious with every Jocelyn's Journey event we held, and it wasn't funny anymore. It is important to Dennis and I that everyone knows: WE MAKE NOTHING ON JOCELYN'S JOURNEY! It is sad to me when I learn about other non-profits paying themselves huge salaries before going to the actual cause they claim to support. Others are giving non-profits a bad name. So, please, let it be known: Dennis and I do not work for RSRT, we do not get paid to have an event and we do not pay the Jocelyn's Journey Committee. We are, truly, a non-profit! Image can also be a struggle!

## The Struggle of Opinions, Not Facts

When Jocelyn was first diagnosed, we visited the "bargaining" phase of grief for a while: *What could I have done differently? What did I do wrong? Why do we deserve this? Why does she deserve this, she is so perfect!*

With Jocelyn not hitting mile stones, followed by her regression, then diagnosis, there had always been the haunting question of "why" which no one could answer. Rett Syndrome occurs 99% of the time as a fluke mutation on the MECP2 gene. When this occurs, it favors no ethnicity, no geographical area, and no economical status. It just happens. It can happen to anyone! Absolutely no preventing that, ever! It was hard for me to grasp, especially after all the "FAILURE" labels and investigations of what I had done wrong during my pregnancy and delivery. There was no rhyme, no reason, we did nothing wrong and we could not have prevented it. I also reasoned that there was no way we were being punished for something either- Dennis and I played our cards right from day one! We were kind, paid our taxes, never killed anyone. We did the stereotypical "right" thing by getting into our careers, buying a home, then getting married and living together... and still, our child had Rett Syndrome. The "why" secretly haunted us in the beginning.

Then, to mix us up even further, the opinions came from others. They were meant to be comforting, but they weren't at all:

"God knew what He was doing giving you a child with Rett Syndrome."

"God knew you could handle this."

"God chose you two to be her parents."

Even Rylee was showing signs of confusion about this topic when she asked me a few months ago, "Mommy, why did Jesus give Jocelyn Rett Syndrome and not me?"

The truth is, when Adam and Eve ate the forbidden fruit, sin entered the world. Before that moment, there was no death, there was no illness, shame or guilt. But, sin is here, and we are all guilty of it. This world is not what it was intended to be, now that sin is here. So there is illness, there is death, there are tears and there is pain. And there will be until Jesus returns. So God didn't give Jocelyn Rett Syndrome, this sinful world did. And Dennis and I did nothing wrong to be given a sick child as well as we couldn't have done anything better to deserve a completely healthy child. It just is what it is. Bad things do not happen to good people, bad things just happen. When parents say, "What did I do to deserve such an awesome child?" the answer is, NOTHING! You didn't earn it! No blessing can be earned.

Now, the exciting part is what was intended for bad, God will use for good and His glory! Jocelyn has Rett Syndrome because there is evil in this world, but we serve an all powerful, all healing God and I know He will use this evil to show His awesomeness to everyone! One of my favorite bible stories is John 9:1-3, "As he passed by, he saw a man blind from birth. And his disciples asked him, 'Rabbi, who sinned, this man or his parents, that he was born bling?' Jesus answered, 'It was not that this man sinned, or his parents, but that the works of God might be displayed in him.'"

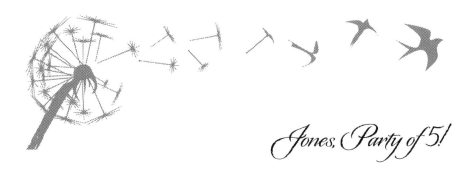

As I mentioned before, I was 6 weeks pregnant with Rylee when Jocelyn was diagnosed. At some point during my first trimester, I remember pushing Jocelyn on the back porch swing while Dennis was barbecuing dinner. It was a calm and peaceful fall evening and our back porch faced the sunset. The beautiful colors of orange, pink, blue and purple filled the sky as the sun tucked behind the mountains.

"This isn't our last pregnancy," I informed Dennis firmly.

"Uhhhh." He didn't know how to respond. "Let's just take things day by day."

I ignored his comment and continued, "We'll have another child after this one. We are taught to prepare for the worst and expect the best. I completely expect the best, that Jocelyn will be cured in just a few years and all of this will be behind us. But, worse case scenario, Jocelyn will not be cured and our second child would then grow up without having a sibling to converse with, complain about how 'mom and dad are being mean'... No, this wont be our last."

Before my second trimester, a CVS (chorionic villus sampling) test was offered to us by Jocelyn's geneticist. (They aspirate and biopsy a sample of the placenta to test.) He informed us that there was a possibility that I carried Rett Syndrome in my ovaries, which would mean any child I had would have Rett Syndrome. The only way to detect this was when I became pregnant again. I started to become very nervous. I had recently learned that Rett was X-linked so typically, only girls had it. I was told that boys with Rett typically don't survive the pregnancy. The possibility of me having Rett in my ovaries filled my throat with a choking guilt for weeks. *I had a miscarriage prior to this pregnancy*, I thought to myself. *What if that was a boy?!* Dennis was adamant to have the CVS done. "I just want to know," he admitted. I honored his wishes, but was extremely hesitant the whole time, because I knew there was a chance of miscarrying when doing the test.

A few weeks after the CVS test, I got a phone call from the geneticist while at work. I ran to the break room to take her call. She calmly said, "The baby is negative for Rett Syndrome." I was so relieved, I felt like I had been holding my breath for 2 weeks! "Do you want to know the gender of the baby," she asked excitedly.

"Yes! Please!"

"It's a girl! Congratulations!"

"Thats great," I said quietly. Tears filled my eyes without control. "Thank you," and I hung up the phone and started to cry. If I wasn't at work, it would've been an ugly cry, but I was trying to keep my make up on and look discrete. Co-workers in the break room with me looked at me like I had just received horrible news. I fought back tears so hard that I felt like my throat was closing.

"I'm fine," managed to escape my mouth.

"Then what's wrong?!" one demanded.

"It's a girl," I whispered.

"That's awesome! Girls are so fun and Jocelyn can play with her!"

My mouth opened and my thoughts poured out without control: "Sure! 'Awesome'?! How am I supposed to raise a healthy girl next to one that isn't. What will Jocelyn think when her sister starts ballet? When her sister wants to do gymnastics. How will I shop for prom and talk boys with my second girl and manage the guilt that Jocelyn wont be a part of it?! Do I hide it from Jocelyn? Do I deprive her younger sister of things that she could do, but her sister can't so 'NO'?! How will Jocelyn feel, seeing Dennis walk her little sister down the isle at her wedding, knowing that she may never get married! When her sister has a baby, and Jocelyn can't. How is this fair to Jocelyn what so ever?!"

Silence filled the room. I saw "deer in headlights" from each of the friends that I had unleashed on. We were all well educated women in the room, but each of us were "Mommies" above all. Not one of them knew how to handle me or what to say. I didn't expect them to. In fact, I was more at ease with their silence and just letting me yell a little. I knew I wouldn't rant like that in front of Dennis. He was probably grieving a little as well. My defensiveness for Jocelyn soon faded with my last tear and last bit of eye make up.

"I'm okay," I broke the silence. "She is healthy, we will be fine. I need to call Dennis." I finally mustered up enough energy to fake smile and call my husband at home, in order to tell him we were having a healthy girl.

Throughout my pregnancy, Jocelyn was still facing challenges and changes. Screaming… the screaming! Some days it was non-stop. We did our best to keep her on a schedule, but nothing seemed to help. Except for the recliner. Thank God for the recliner. I remember rocking her in the morning, in between therapy sessions in the afternoon, then again in the evening. Sometimes she fell asleep, sometimes we both did. During my last trimester, we would rock and rock and Rylee would get in on some of the action. She would kick Jocelyn's hand, which was resting on my belly. Jocelyn's look of amazement at me was priceless. It was like any other 2 year old who knew there was a baby in her mommy's tummy. The three of us started to bond this way and I will cherish those days always.

After delivery and recovery from Rylee, when Dennis went back to work, our hours in the recliner continued. I was nursing Rylee close to me and right next to her, I'd drape Jocelyn over my lap and "hand-over-hand" give her a bottle, since she didn't have enough control of her hands to hold it on her own. Yes, Jocelyn was still on a bottle at 3 years old, it's how she got most of her nutrition before the G-tube. The miles we put on that recliner were record breaking. The snuggles, priceless.

When Rylee switched to a bottle around 7 months, we would continue with the same routine. For a few weeks I had to "double fist" bottles, hand-over-hand with Jocelyn and completely hold Rylee's bottle by myself, while she did something adorable, like play with her feet or her sister's hair. The first night when Rylee reached and held her bottle on her own, I was sad at first, but quickly became relieved! I helped her and encouraged her to hold it on her own every feed thereafter. It only took a few days before Rylee began feeding herself independently. I was amazed at how quickly she had mastered that skill, and never lost it. She still laid all over Jocelyn and I, to get her snuggles in.

Rylee was so easy! She would feed, fairly quickly even, sit herself up and let out a burp. It took months for Dennis and I not to jump when Rylee burped, expecting a spit up. We were so used to Jocelyn, her entire life, where a burp meant a mess of regurgitated food. We would anticipate and grab a burp cloth or a towel with Rylee, but never needed it. I remember Dennis saying, "Wow, if this is how it's supposed to be, we can have like 10 more kids!"

Rylee hit all of her milestones on time. When she sat, she sat and never really needed help. She "superman'd" on her belly for a few weeks, then it turned to creeping, then a crawl. Dennis and I were absolutely amazed. I'm not sure how Jocelyn felt about it. When I gave them both tummy time on the carpet to play, Rylee would do her scoot or crawl over to her sister and Jocelyn would smile at the attention and sudden company. Rylee would give her kisses, play with her hair; sometimes pull it. Jocelyn would get angry and give her little sister an annoying stink eye. It was adorable to watch them interact. Even when Jocelyn got irritated with her, it felt normal. Rylee brought normalcy to us. Our family was moving forward in the direction of happiness and out of the darkness. The idea of a second girl became fun, towards the end of my pregnancy, but it was moments like this when Rylee loved on her sister that I was truly relieved that we had had a girl and not a boy. Rylee just seemed to have a loving, gentle nature about her when it came to Jocelyn. I was having fun and I loved every moment with my girls!

When Dennis and I decided to start trying for a second child, we thought it would help Jocelyn progress and catch up on milestones. This idea was pre-diagnosis, but our hope did, in fact, happen! One day during one of Jocelyn's in home therapy sessions, we were trying to get Jocelyn to say "ladybug". Jocelyn had verbalized it a few times before, during one of our many hours in the rocking chair. I had a coffee mug with ladybugs on it. I saw her staring at it continuously so I simply told her what it was. She then repeated me: "la-dy bu". With Rett Syndrome, sometimes the stars align just right or, if the girl really REALLY wants to blurt something out, it can happen! However, it is extremely difficult for them to do on demand. Still, to encourage it and to work on it is essential, regardless of success.

During this therapy session, the therapist and I got out a lady bug pillow to encourage Jo to say it. By this time Rylee was pulling up to stand and getting into absolutely everything. "Reckless RyRy" I'd call her. So we were playing with Jocelyn's ladybug and Rylee decided she wanted it. She barged her way over and started to take the pillow from Jocelyn's therapy area. Laughing I spoke for Jocelyn, as I sometimes do: "Say, 'no no Ryry!'"

And Jocelyn obliged, clear as day, "NO! NO! RY! RY!" I was in shock and so proud. Rylee looked confused as to what was going on. The therapist and I cheered and cheered for the annoyed Jocelyn who verbalized exactly what she wanted to say! Thankfully, I caught this on video and captured the moment. (It's on YouTube if you're curious https://youtu.be/_TVvopjy-tA)

This wasn't the only time Rylee helped with therapy. A little after she turned one, I was so exhausted from being in the house all of the time doing in home therapy. I felt bad for Rylee as well. We never had time to go to the park, visit with friends, or just do "normal" things. But therapy was important for Jo and it was helping her! Finally, I found a "mommy and me" gymnastics at a gym down the street from us. I got approval for the therapist to join us and be Jocelyn's "mommy" for class and I would chase little Rylee around and be her "mommy" for class. It was a lot of fun and both the girls really enjoyed it. So did the therapist and I. Everything was hand over hand with Jocelyn. We modified as much as we could for her, but tried to make sure she was still having fun. Some of the other kids would look curiously at Jocelyn. Moms would watch me and smile a reassuring smile and tried to make sure their child was considerate of Jocelyn. It was a great time the few months we were there. However, the desert heat in the summer became more than what Jocelyn could bare. There was no air conditioning in the gym and she would just sweat and complain the entire session. So we stopped going all together.

Rylee's nurturing nature became evident at a very young age. The winter when she was just two years old, four year old Jocelyn became pretty sick. She had a cough for two days, but then, she stopped coughing. She ate nothing and drank very little of her bottle. This illness was pre

G-tube, so I had no way of getting fluid or nutrition in Jocelyn without her cooperation. I'm not sure if it was the nurse in me, or the mommy, but I just knew, something wasn't right with Jocelyn. Dennis was at work and I was striving to find a sitter for Rylee, while packing a bag of usual supplies to take Jocelyn to the emergency room. Rylee knew something was wrong and she followed me all over the house. All I could explain, which she would understand was, "Sissy has an owee."

"Oh, no! Sissy owee?" she asked in her adorable voice and limited vocabulary.

"Yes baby. It's okay though. Mama's going to fix it," I reassured her while hiding my panic. I just knew she had pneumonia. I busily packed while praying it wasn't too bad of a case. After a few minutes without a shadow, I started searching the house for curious Rylee. I went to the living room where Jocelyn was sleeping, right where I left her, half naked to cool her fever. But I noticed some new accessories all over her frail body. Rylee had covered Jocelyn in bandaids! I found Rylee in her bathroom looking for more bandaids to add to the half box she already used on her sister.

"Sissy owee bye-bye," she informed me proudly.

"Thank you Rylee. You are such a good girl!" And that broke me! I cried and let myself calm down a minute. I was grateful I had such a thoughtful two year old, who was doing everything in her power to help her sister wake up and feel better.

That night, Jocelyn was admitted to the hospital with pneumonia on both sides of her lungs. They treated her with an IV, oxygen when needed, antibiotics, and breathing treatments. During the breathing treatments, the respiratory therapist gave us a tiny plastic tool to percuss Jocelyn's chest with. It seemed to small, but the adult tool seemed so large. The respiratory therapist gave us both allowing us to decide which one worked best for Jocelyn. When we were finally discharged, two days later, Rylee was thrilled that we brought her home a chest percussion tool, for her to use, while we continued to percuss Jocelyn. Everyone got percussed once she figured out how to use it. Rylee percussed her dolls, my chest, Dennis' head. She loved being a part of the treatment plan. Moreover, she was happy her sister was finally home and looking better. Just as Dennis and I were baffled at Rylee meeting milestones as a baby, we were just as baffled at her level of understanding and problem solving at such a young age. She was our ray of light in the middle of a storm.

When Rylee's vocabulary grew, along with her understanding, she began to realize, something was different with her sister.

"Is Sissy a baby?" She would ask. "When I was a baby, did I have Rett Syndrome?"

Questions were sometimes difficult to answer, especially in front of Jocelyn. I always tried to have a positive spin on things under debate, so Jocelyn could hear that I still believed that she could do everything her sister could do.

I started to notice Rylee starving for other kids to play with her. I feared that our limitations at home were holding her back from what she needed. Once Jocelyn started Kindergarten, we put Rylee in preschool. Rylee flourished. She absolutely loved it and never had anxiety about me dropping her off. It almost made me sad, but I got over it quickly. She was obviously very independent and I almost felt responsible for that quality. Ever since the first time she grabbed that bottle and held it on her own, I pushed her to be independent. It was a survival technique, I suppose, in our home.

Just before Rylee turned 3, I swallowed my defense for Jocelyn and enrolled her in ballet. She loved it and Jocelyn didn't seem to mind at all when her sister was in dance class and she sat with me in the parent area. Jocelyn seemed to like the one on one time with me, and I with her. I knew in the back of my mind, however, that Jocelyn wanted to be in there dancing too. Around that time, on career day at school, using her Tobii eye gaze communication device, Jocelyn said that she wanted to be a ballerina when she grew up. I would occasionally remind Jocelyn that she too, would be in dance class one day. And that is why we have our Jocelyn's Journey events- to get her a cure!

Christmas of 2014, Dennis decided it was time to get 4 year old Rylee, a "big girl bike". One with training wheels that would accommodate her long legs. I immediately protested, "No, that's not fair! We can't get Jo a bike. So Rylee doesn't get one either."

"Well, that's not fair to Rylee," Dennis argued. A good point. I was quiet when we went shopping and I secretly hoped the toy store had run out of bikes.

Shopping for Jocelyn has always been difficult. She cannot manipulate toys that are of an appropriate age for her, so she usually gets clothes, jewelry or movies. We loaded up at the toy store then went to the bike section. Dennis picked out a bike for Rylee and we made our way up to the front of the store to pay. I was almost in a panic, I was so disgusted with our situation. I was praying and praying in line for an idea. An idea for an awesome gift for Jocelyn that was just as cool as a bike, but something she could use and manipulate. My mind was a blank. Tears welled up in my eyes while our turn to check out began creeping closer and closer. Dennis noticed the tidal waves about to burst out of my eyes, "Knock it off, Elizabeth! Rylee needs a childhood too!" he scolded me. I knew he was right, but my heart was breaking with sympathetic envy for Jocelyn. There are bikes that are "special needs" or "adaptive equipment bikes" which Jocelyn could be able to ride, but they are thousands of dollars. Something we didn't have lying around, especially on one income.

The next day I prayed and prayed for an idea. I went to a Rett Syndrome Facebook group and asked for help for an idea. Many people related to our situation and my heart ache. Some posted replies of what they were getting their Rett girl, trying to help come up with ideas for Jocelyn. One man's simple reply stuck out, "Try Red Star Ridders". Without hesitation, I did a search on Red Star Ridders and found a website. It was a non-profit organization which helped special needs children get adaptive bikes. I honestly felt horrible asking for help. We fundraise for Jocelyn's Journey and support RSRT for a lot of money every year. It just felt awkward for me to ask someone for more! Then I recognized the feeling that was coming over me; the fear of what people would think of me, shame, guilt... I immediately disregarded all of those feelings and submitted our family story to the website through a "contact us" e-mail button. I had doubts that anything would come of it, but it was a guarantee "nothing" if I didn't try. So I submitted and continued to brainstorm for more ideas.

The next day someone from Red Star Riders called me. She was a sweet therapist who said she loved our story and was inspired to help Jocelyn get a bike for Christmas. I was in disbelief speaking with her! Not only did she call me, but she wanted to help. This time Dennis wasn't around to tell me not to let the flood gates to my eyes swing wide open. She said she happened to have a cancelation that day at 1p.m. and if I could

Elizabeth Jones

bring Jocelyn to them in Los Angeles, there was a team there that could try and help us. The sweet lady said it was incredible that the cancelation had just happened because they were usually weeks out on appointments. THANK YOU, GOD!

I immediately pulled Jocelyn out of school and we zoomed down to Los Angeles. There was a team of therapists there to design a bike that would accommodate Jocelyn. Measurements, bikes there for her to try, different sizes... and they were all so kind. When Jocelyn wasn't around I asked the therapists if they could try not to get Jocelyn's hopes up and keep referring to "if" she could get a bike. They were great and went along with it. They started saying how they were Santa's helpers and they needed to give him design plans for a bike, just in case he had time to make one for her. Jocelyn ate up every word and every ounce of attention. She was in such a good mood and cooperated nicely. Once the team designed the bike, they then said that they would do fundraising for us and try to find a sponsor to pay for Jocelyn's bike. We thanked them and went home.

I shared on social media what had happened, from the toy store getting Rylee's bike to Jocelyn possibly getting a bike donated. The response was incredible. Everyone enjoyed our Christmas story and some said, "This is what Christmas is about!" It was so refreshing to spread Christmas joy, hope, belief, and my favorite, Jocelyn's excited smile!

Two days later, the same therapist from Red Star Riders called me and said they had found a sponsor for Jocelyn's bike. This gentleman paid for 100% of the balance after mine and Dennis' donation. I was crying with excitement and disbelief of the events that had rapidly took place over the past week.

"This is a total God thing," I explained to the lady.

She replied, "I hope you don't mind me saying so, but after reading your e-mail and talking with you, I have the strongest sense of God's favor all over you and your family. I know He has great things for you guys." I was completely speechless. All I could do was cry. I was so grateful for Jocelyn's Christmas miracle.

I didn't keep this to myself. I had to spread the joy and share on social media. It was exciting to see everyone else as excited as us. Sharing Christmas joy is all I thought I was doing, but God took it a step further.

A local bike shop, Victorville Cycles, heard about our story on Facebook and offered to assemble the new bike when it arrived! That worked out beautifully since Christmas was only a few days away and Dennis was working most of them. Special needs bikes are complex to assemble too. Everything worked out so beautifully!

Christmas morning came and I took a million pictures and videos of both Jocelyn and Rylee getting bikes from Santa that morning. Both the girl's faces were so priceless when they came to the tree and saw their bikes! It was the best gift for all of us! We rode all over inside the house then outside as well. We still ride often, and both the girls are making huge progress on their big girl bikes! So blessed!

In the summer of 2015, Dennis and I decided that if we were going to have a third child, we had better start soon. Jocelyn was getting heavier and I was worried if we waited, she'd be too heavy for me to carry while I was pregnant. So we decided to go for it. Finally, I got to tell Dennis we were expecting in a Christmas present. It was a picture frame with 3 windows. In window #1 was Jocelyn, #2 was Rylee, and #3 was a picture of the positive test! I was proud of my creativity. I wanted something special for my last time telling my husband that we were expecting.

I'll be honest, we were hoping for a boy. At my 18 week ultrasound, they brought Dennis in the room at the end and the tech said, "Congratulations, it's a girl!" Dennis was more surprised than I.

"I want to name her Abigail and we can call her 'Abbie' after my grandpa, AB," I informed Dennis. Poor guy didn't have a chance to digest any of what was going on and now I was already naming her. In the end, obviously, I got my way.

I had a rough pregnancy with Abigail, probably because I was much older than my first two pregnancies. When I started to get really worried about Abbie, I gave her to God. Yep, *Let your will be done!* And that was it. I struggled a few times when I'd start worrying again, but then I reminded myself, that she was Gods and all would work out.

One morning before school, I was sitting with Jocelyn waiting for her bus and Abbie became very active in my belly. I put Jo's hand on my belly and she got so excited. "Ahhhh Buhhh!" Jocelyn exclaimed. I was so proud of her, being able to say her baby sister's name. It was priceless and I was thrilled I got it on camera. And that remains one of Abbie's nick names, "Ah Buh".

Bringing Abigail home from the hospital was precious. Jocelyn was so excited but had been down this road before. Rylee's eyes lit up and she immediately asked if Abigail could sleep in her room. It has been so fun watching the two older girls love their baby sister. Our home became a circus again during Abbie's first year of life, with Jocelyn having surgery and Dennis and I trying to meet the demands of each of our girls. But it was fun and we knew that this time was short.

Like with Rylee, with every mile stone Abigail hit and never lost amazed us. We aren't the parents that talk about how sad they are that their child is growing up too fast. We feel extremely blessed when our children advance, because we have lived the alternative of a child never hitting some mile stones.

Watching Abigail follow her big sister Rylee around the house is the cutest thing. Hearing Rylee tell me every night how adorable Abigail is warms my heart. Watching them bond is an honor that I get to witness every day. Abbie loves playing in Rylee's room while Rylee dances around singing to her music. Abbie attempts to join in on all the ballet moves Rylee has mastered. Again, wanting a boy initially, I am overwhelmed with joy that Abigail is a girl. My girls are great together.

Abbie is still trying to figure Jocelyn out. Abbie tries so hard to get to Jocelyn's feeding tube, at least twice a day. She thinks it is a toy. So we have to watch them closely. When Jocelyn is on the floor, Abbie loves to crawl over to her, sit on her, and grab at her. Jocelyn is incredibly patient with her curious baby sister. Abbie has to repeatedly be told to "be nice" as she tries to pick on Jocelyn's eyes, ears and nose. I've even caught Abbie's entire hand in Jocelyn's mouth and Jocelyn just takes the beating and laughs about it. Jo has never bit Abbie, not yet, knock on wood.

Recently, one evening when all of our girls were in bed, Dennis and I were sitting on the couch talking. We started comparing the three of our girls as babies, trying to decide who looked like who. As I reflected on my first baby, I realized how much I missed her. Then a revelation came to me.

"Dennis, you know what I just realized? I've been trying to get my

Baby Jo back, but she's gone. Theres no going back, there's no getting her back. I know Jocelyn is 8 and is mature like an 8 year old. I always want people to talk to her and treat her like an 8 year old, not like a baby. But somewhere, deep inside, I think I've been wanting my Baby Jo back, and I can't have her... that time has passed and we missed it." Dennis and I both wiped a few tears and accepted that painful truth. Then we gratefully tucked each of our girls in, and went to bed.

*Journeymen*

The few years of Jocelyn's life, of her journey, were pretty typical of other Rett Syndrome girls. A beautiful, seemingly healthy baby, who typically grows into a toddler, hitting some or most milestones. Then, it seems as if overnight, the happy, normal progressing toddler is left with a body she can no longer control like she used to. It is said that terrible two's occur because the child is frustrated, trying to get what he or she wants. Usually it is lack of communication that increases the frustration. So during a time when it is typically normal for a child to become frustrated, Rett Syndrome girls also struggle with losing fine motor skills, some gross motor skills, and many of their verbal communication skills, which they had acquired over their lives.

Most Rett Syndrome families I've met have had a similar story to Jocelyn's when it came to getting diagnosed. Doctor after doctor, specialist after specialist, months and even years before getting a diagnosis. I've seen too, the more high functioning the girl, the harder it is to diagnosis because the medical field hasn't caught up to Rett research, knowing that Rett Syndrome has a very wide spectrum. Or, like in Jocelyn's case, she was not showing the typical Rett Syndrome signs, hand wringing or hand washing. This threw off some of the doctors, and caused them not to order the test sooner. Before the DNA blood test for Rett Syndrome in 1999, this was how the girls were diagnosed. Symptom based.

What is hard to imagine is before the blood test, high functioning girls that were not hand washing or having other "classic" signs of Rett Syndrome were not diagnosed. They were undoubtedly "different" from other children, and "delayed," but unbeknownst to their parents, the girl was cognitive, understanding the world around her, but unable to interact with it. In the world back then, the majority of these girls were more than likely institutionalized. Possibly sitting in wheelchairs at a young age with little verbal skills and without hope. This absolutely breaks my heart.

Having a child with Rett Syndrome during any era is difficult. However, I feel extremely blessed that we are raising Jocelyn in todays world. A world with RSRT, and their innovative research, and a team of the best world wide research doctors who collaborate and work vigorously to cure this disease. Besides the prestigious doctors, and RSRT becoming a $36 million organization in just 6 years, everyone you encounter with RSRT, from Monica to the researchers, everyone is full of integrity and compassion. They are absolutely down to earth, and are just as excited to meet a new Rett Syndrome girl as the parents are to meet them! I couldn't imagine raising Jocelyn without the hope they have brought to us.

I look back on Jocelyn's diagnosis journey and wonder about other undiagnosed girls. "Just have a doctor write down that she has Cerebral Palsy," I was told on more than one occasion. I refused. But how many parents didn't refuse and complied with this clerk's request; only wanting what was best for their daughter and doing what they were told in order to get her the help she needed. How many girls are out there, of all ages, sitting at home or in nursing homes, completely cognitive and aware, but no one talks to them age appropriately because they were misdiagnosed. I think of these girls, knowing that a cure is coming, and soon. What about them? When Jocelyn is cured of Rett Syndrome and walking around, giggling and playing with her sisters, these girls are left untreated.

What about the Rett Syndrome girls in the future? The babies who are not even born yet? Rett Syndrome is more prevalent than some of the diseases and syndromes that are screened for when babies are just a few days old. Mostly, because early intervention for these syndromes and diseases gives best possible outcomes, AND because there are treatments available. So if Rett Syndrome is more prevalent than some of these, once there is a cure, I feel we should screen for Rett Syndrome as well.

Early intervention and treatment would be ideal! Not to mention, screening at birth would prevent misdiagnoses. Post cure, if there was a Rett Syndrome girl labeled as "failure to thrive" as a baby, just as Jocelyn was, then aggressive treatment for failure to thrive, such as TPN or G-tube… all of that would be an unnecessary bandaid to the true problem- Rett Syndrome. It would be more ideal to treat Rett Syndrome than to have all of the expensive, unnecessary tests Jocelyn and other Rett Syndrome girls endure over their lifetime.

What about SIDs? "Sudden Infant Death Syndrome". Jocelyn's monitor went off all of the time as an infant. I have taken care of newborns in the ER who have apneic spells- they stop breathing. When you witness a newborn having an apenic spell, you stimulate them to encourage a breath. Well if Jocelyn was in her basinet having apneic spells when her monitor went off, Dennis and I stimulated her by picking her up. Quiet possibly it was her reflux causing her difficulty and therefore holding her breath. But in either case, we feel fortunate to have escaped a tragic outcome, because of the SIDs monitor. However, Rett Syndrome girls are at risk for "sudden and unexplained death". Isn't this the same as SIDs, only they aren't infants anymore? Perhaps there is a connection. Perhaps not. But if Rett Syndrome were on the newborn screening test, and treatment were available, perhaps the incidences of SIDs would also decline.

My point is, even after Jocelyn is cured, there is still so much work to be done. Jocelyn's Journey will continue, post cure. I am not sure what direction it will take first, I am confident that God will guide my steps and show me where and when to move. For now, step one, WE NEED THE CURE!

Over our journey the past seven years, I have learned that Jocelyn's Journey is about so much more than Jocelyn. It's about her Rett sisters too, getting their cure right along side of her. It's about the girls of the future who will be diagnosed. Remember, Rett Syndrome occurs at random- it can happen to anyone's sweet little baby. That is scary. But replace that fear with hope. We are close!

We are currently planning for our 6th annual Jocelyn's Journey event. Like I said earlier, it's like planning a wedding every year on a $0 budget. So yes, it can be stressful, but it is so worth it. To not host an event and to not support RSRT, I would be rolling over, waving a white flag and allowing Rett Syndrome consume us. I just cannot bring myself to do that. I will fight back and we will win! Something that the Rett community says that I live by is "My daughter has Rett Syndrome, Rett Syndrome does not have her." And it will never HAVE her!

Over the past two years I have tried to take a step back to see the bigger picture of Jocelyn's Journey. My first revelation of this came from the innermost circle first- the Jocelyn's Journey Committee. The committee consists mostly of my high school friends and a few family members. We start in January, gathering once a month to start planning our event, which is usually in October. The beginning of the year we are relaxed but by August, we all have our game faces on. However, every month, it is a bit of a social gathering with purpose. We have snacks, visit and have a few laughs. It is adult time which I look forward to. And some months, it is the only evening I get any kind of social interaction. I know that the committee enjoys our time together as well. I am completely humbled by their eagerness to help with the event. I absolutely could not do it without their help. Some months, Rett strikes our family hard, with Jocelyn getting sick or changes at school needing to be done. I could easily become stressed. Those months, the committee gives me grace, steps in and helps run the meeting smoothly and whatever needed to get done, gets done. I absolutely couldn't have an event without them.

Looking back on our first two years together as a committee, I remember being puzzled as to why they were so dedicated to us. Why was Jocelyn's Journey so important to them? I knew why I was doing it, it was obvious, I was funding the cure to save my daughter's life. But why would my friends be so passionate about it as well? Eyes off myself and my selfish motives, I began to realize what it meant to them.

There has been pain and there has been suffering within our committee. We are a committee, a team. No one is alone, we fight side by side! Our committee is full of incredible people, mostly women, who have struggled with being victims of adultery, divorce, loss of multiple unborn children, and even domestic violence. Some have lost loved ones to tragedy, cancer, or other diseases. All of these things can make a woman feel helpless and hopeless. One committee member has actually experienced loss to Rett Syndrome within her family, her cousins daughter went with God at the age of 8 years. (Sweet Jayda, Jocelyn's Journey is in honor of you too! We fight for all the Rett Syndrome victims, those who will get the earthly cure, and the ones who received the ultimate, eternal cure). Jocelyn's Journey is a safe place for each of these women to fight back, to find hope, to find worth. Every October, we are all rewarded for our efforts as we celebrate another successful year.

Some of the committee members don't have children and therefore are eager to help advocate for mine. Then there are others who have children around Jocelyn's age; I was pregnant with Jocelyn with some of them. Perhaps being on the committee satisfies a bit of "survivor's guilt", knowing that Rett Syndrome strikes at random and we very well could be hosting an event in their daughters name instead of Jocelyn's. I am humbled for their help and they know, if tables were turned, I would be on their committee as well. I can't help but think, now, of what my friends had gone through watching my family suffer for so many years. Watching mine and Dennis' heart break a little more every day as we struggled with the horrible question, "What's wrong with my baby?" While the sin of disease consumed me and filled my heart with more sinful, ugly feelings of hate, envy, the selfish "why me?" question. My friends stood by and had to watch. Wanting to help me, but not knowing how. Probably afraid to try at times. My heart was so uninviting and ugly. Looking back, even the first two years of hosting Jocelyn's Journey, I had an "It's all about me and my family" attitude. Still a bit guarded and jealous at that time. Thank God my friends had compassion for me and returned every year. The past two years, I have strived to make it about everyone, not just Jocelyn and my family.

Two years ago, the Jocelyn's Journey Committee launched a sub committee, the Jocelyn's Journey Junior Committee. It consists of the children of all the committee members. Most of these peers are right around Jocelyn's age and they are so excited and eager to help! McKenzie, the little baby I was so jealous of, when Jocelyn wasn't progressing along with her, is on the junior committee, developing leadership skills. I am so touched to see her helping heart do what she can to help her friend. Last year, the week of the event, she emptied out her piggy bank and gave her mom, Crystal, her very last dime. "Here," she instructed, "put this toward's Jocelyn's medicine." It's so sweet to watch her empathy for her peer and her wanting to help.

We also often see Jacob, my other matron of honor's baby who is Jocelyn's age. When he comes over he is a sweet kid who waves at Jo and says "hi," then goes running around to play with the kids, just as typical 8 year old boys do. What he doesn't see is Jocelyn glowing (almost flirting) when he says hi to her. Melts my heart that she is a little flirt.

Erica is one of the older girls on the junior committee who had an immediate love for Jocelyn from day one. It is precious how supportive Erica is and how concerned she is with Jocelyn getting her cure soon! She wears her Jocelyn's Journey shirt once a week to school and develops writing assignments around Jocelyn's Journey, Rett Syndrome, and how she is helping to save the world.

Last but not least, a junior committee member I'd like to tell you about is London. London goes to school with Jocelyn and I remember the first day we met her. It was the first day of 1st grade and she was so curious of Jocelyn. She watched Jo intently and followed us around at lunch and at recess. When Jo's paraeducator at the time and I engaged London in conversation with Jocelyn, that was it. Instant BFF's (best friends forever). When I was at school with Jocelyn, London was sure to be by her side. Teachers told me of the bond they noticed between the two girls and how they were good together. Jocelyn having a friend like London feels like winning the lottery to a special needs parent. Since diagnosis, I've always been defensive of Jo and strived to show the world how she is an ordinary 8 year old. A pure heart like London, there was never any convincing needed. She has loved my daughter from the start, and Jocelyn lights up even at the mention of her name.

I am so appreciative of mainstreaming at school. Mainstreaming is the special education students going into the general education classroom for a period of time per day. This builds relationships between the kids and prevents segregation. It is good for all of the kids, as it prepares them to deal with all types of people and work and live with them, despite differences, just as they are going to have to in adulthood. It's so sweet to see all of the kids interact with Jocelyn. Ms. Super Sara keeps track of who's turn it is to push Jocelyn in her wheelchair at recess. To say the least, Jocelyn is pretty popular at school.

I am so proud of the Jocelyn's Journey Junior Committee and all the children who interact Jocelyn. It is the hope of all of the parents on the

Jocelyn's Journey Committee that our children are learning to help others and that they have the power to change the world.

Jocelyn's Journey stretches even beyond the committee. It is an amazing experience to go into a business with a Jocelyn's Journey homemade flyer and tell our story and watch people get excited to help with donated goods, coupons… anything. There are many, MANY times the manager, or person I am speaking with, has a relatable struggle. The owner of a local frozen yogurt shop had recently lost his son and was gracious to help our event. A local jeweler, who donates every year, has become a friend, and he loves Jocelyn and expects a visit from us at least every year. On at least three different occasions, we've met restaurant managers who were eager and delighted to help with our event because they related to our struggles, having a child with autism themselves. Our BrittleNut friend is gracious with her donations- she lost a beautiful little girl to SIDs. The list goes on, and on, and on. One conversation (yes, "soliciting") gives an opportunity for strangers to become friends, and is a chance for them to tell their story, a chance for them to feel hope and, again a chance to fight back.

One of my favorite encounters occurred the day before the 4th event. I was having trouble with our event brochure, which advertised for all of our sponsors. It was important to me to get it right because I am always worried about making sure we thank everyone appropriately. When I attempted to e-mail the 6+page brochure to the woman who prints them, she was receiving the pages upside down and out of order. I had a full morning, a meeting at Jocelyn's school, reviewing Nanea's video for the event, and Jocelyn's Journey was being introduced at the Apple Valley Chamber of Commerce luncheon, where I had to speak about our event. The printer was all the way across town, but I had to go in and show her the exact layout. I zoomed over, between appointments, and the sweet lady and I cut out and stapled a sample for her to follow. As we were organizing the brochure, she started asking what Jocelyn's Journey was. So I shared my 2 minute story about Rett Syndrome and why fundraising was so important for the research. She hung on every word and became tearful. She commended me for my efforts to help my daughter, then pointed to a picture on her desk. The picture was of two adult men, her sons. She explained that one was a police officer and the other was disabled. As she pointed to her disabled son, she began telling her story but talking about him in past tense. She spoke as if it had happened yesterday. All of the doctors visits, tests, procedures, poking and prodding on her baby from the time he was one year old. She shared her story with me and now I was the one chocked up. I felt divine alignments right then and there, as I now hung on every word. She said they never found out what was wrong, but she loved him so much, just the same. As any parent would.

Almost embarrassed, she ended her story. "I'm sorry, I didn't meant to go on and on like that. We lost my son a few years back and it still feels so recent."

I thanked her for sharing with me and I wanted to hear everything she had to share. She wiped tears away and smiled the sweetest smile. As I departed, we shook hands over a tall counter that separated us. I wanted to hug her, but the strong hand shake between us two moms, empowering each other was enough. I felt her love and she felt mine. It was a memorable moment for me and touched me so much. My busy day of appointments and errands didn't matter anymore because I felt with every fiber, I was right where God wanted me to be. This incredible woman needed to tell her story, and I was honored to hear it.

A few months ago, Dennis and I hired a fellow firefighter, he works with, to steam clean our carpets. He runs his own business as a side job. While he was working, he and Dennis got to talking. Dennis shared Jocelyn's story about Rett Syndrome and his fire brother listened with true compassion and empathy. He had a family member who suffered with autism, and he was relating to how it could be hard on the family. "Anything I can do to help" he offered in support of Jocelyn's Journey. I was so appreciative of his help and support, and it reminded me of how much I love our family being a part of the fire family! It truly is a band of brothers (and some sisters) who help and support each other.

Both Dennis' union (San Bernardino County Firefighters IAFF local 935) and association (San Bernardino County Firefighters Association) have been one of our most consistent sponsors of Jocelyn's Journey! It humbles me to see so many familiar fire faces at our event and their willingness to support us and help us. Dennis and I do what we can when there are others in our fire family who need help, have fundraisers for a sick child or other family member. Without question, even on tight months, we donate and support whenever opportunity arises. It's a family, it's just what we do. I am honored to be a part of it.

Sometimes the biggest lessons I've learned are when I am trying to teach my children something. One morning, Rylee asked, "Mommy, if we are having Jocelyn's Journey, when is my journey?"

I tried to explain it as best I could to my young daughter, "Ry, it's not just Jocelyn's journey, it's everyone's journey, it's just called "Jocelyn's Journey'. It's about everyone, not just Jo."

I meant every word! Jocelyn's Journey is not just about Jocelyn and her immediate family, it's about every Rett Syndrome girl and their families, all of Jocelyn's Journey Committee, the sponsors, our gala guests every year, all our donators and supporters, every person who we share our story with, and now YOU! We are all a part of it, "Journeyman" of Jocelyn's Journey, and I am thrilled and honored to be on it with you!

A new vision for Jocelyn's Journey came to me in late 2015. I would like our cause to be a bigger part of the community. The committee and I strive to go to events within our community, while we all wear our matching Jocelyn's Journey t-shirts to spread awareness, initiate conversation… "living loud" I call it. I feel the push to spread the word and get the Jocelyn's Journey name out there. This was new territory for me and I had to seek wisdom. One of our consistent supporters, Casey Armstrong at Armstrong Fairway Insurance, took Jocelyn's Journey underwing and helped us get into the community effectively! (Thank you Casey! You have been a wonderful friend, supporter and have been a huge help in growing our event!)

My first big event was at Granite Hills High School The same students who cater our Jocelyn's Journey event every year chose us as a topic for a leadership competition called Skills USA. I was thrilled and eager to help and talk with the team at the drop of a hat. Part of their project required educating their student body about their topic. So they invited me to speak at an assembly. An assembly with over 600 people! I was incredibly nervous at first, but it was actually a really good experience. All of the kids were respectful and listened intently to our story and our event. They even got to meet Jocelyn who was hanging out with Super Sara on the side of the room.

Another awesome event is a Pig Roast held by committee member, Crystal Esquivel's, dad and step-mom. Crystal's parents have generously supported Jocelyn's Journey since the first year through Ripley and Associates Law firm, where they work. They wanted to do more, however. So they decided to have a barbecue in honor of Jocelyn's Journey. Rosie, Crystal's step-mom, tells her friends that they are "feeding the need right in their own back yard" referring to our non-profit as the need. It is a fun, simple evening that exposes Jocelyn's Journey to a group of people I would otherwise had never met. This past year we raised over $3,000 and two families became gala sponsors. Such an incredible blessing to know such wonderful people and to meet new incredible people! Thank you Gerry and Rosie!

The butterfly effect of networking never ceases to amaze me. (Undoubtedly God's hand is always in on it!) I was invited to judge a talent show at a local high school. It was incredibly fun and I met so many new people. One of which, was the former mayor's wife! We got to talking and enjoyed our visit. A few months later, she contacted me to speak at an event called "Ignite". There were 12 speakers who each spoke on something they were passionate about. Each speaker had 5 minutes to speak on 20 slides to a room of 200 guests. It was intense and a lot of fun and 200 more people heard about Rett Syndrome and Jocelyn's Journey who had never heard of it before. It was a great night.

But the butterfly effect didn't stop there. One of the 12 speakers was Assemblyman Jay Obernolte. I got to meet him and we chatted for a few minutes. It was pretty amazing and I appreciated how approachable our district's elected official was. It made me less nervous to keep the conversation going. Much to my surprise, 5 months later, I got a call from Sacramento explaining that the Assemblyman chose Jocelyn's Journey as our districts non-profit of 2016! I was floored with shock! My friend and committee member Heather, flew up to Sacramento for pictures and an award presentation and lunch with the Assemblyman. An incredible experience and a mind-blowing title Jocelyn's Journey received, "Non-Profit of the Year!" Just WOW!

Perhaps why God called me to write this book was to bring more awareness about Rett Syndrome so when there is a cure, it will inspire more people to believe in miracles.

Maybe this book is intended for the friends and family of someone who has Rett Syndrome. So you could have a peek into the lives of what your loved ones are going through. Maybe you will learn how you can help them. A recommendation: Ask the parents how their marriage is and ask how you could help. Marriage is a struggle even without a sick child. Help your loved ones by learning about Rett and their specific issues. Ask how you can help. Help by giving the parents or caregiver a break. Not just by watching them at night when the work is all done. Step in at the hour of the storm and send the parent to the movies. One day away, even a few hours, could refuel their jets for an entire week.

Maybe this book is to bring awareness to our voiceless victims. They are beautiful people, trapped in their bodies. Could you imagine? Try to imagine… I bet your day just looked a whole lot better than your imagined Rett life, right? Treat them and speak to them, age appropriately. Some may not be able to look you directly in the eye, but they hear you.

Or perhaps God called me to write and share, in order to help so many of my fellow Rett parents, who I see struggling every day on social media. I see posts of parents feeling alone, how no one understands, how they envy "typical" children and sometimes hate to be around them. I've seen posts where parents struggle with faith, doubting God and asking what they did wrong to have their child suffer with this horrible Rett monster. Parents post of fear- fear has to be the most frustrating thing to see from my fellow Rett parents. It paralyzes them, just as it did me. Specifically, I remember a recent post about a mother terrified her child will die during the night and she wont know it. A few replies down on this post, another parent explained how she avoids this: her and her husband take turns sleeping with their Rett girl, every night! That absolutely breaks my heart. Their marriage has to be suffering over that! And what guilt and blame would come of that if God were to take the child home during the night while one or the other laid next to her. But I remember being there- paralyzed by that fear. Before I surrendered to Jesus I was so worried about the same thing and I searched and searched for help. My cocktail to even fall asleep rotated between a few drinks, an antihistamine, or prescribed anti-anxitey medication! And the worst part, none of them worked. But guess what did- Jesus! I now sleep like a baby and have the best energy in the morning to be the best mom God has called me to be, not a tired, sleep deprived grouch coming off of sedatives.

Rett Syndrome is a result of this earth being filled with sin! Disease is an attack on people, to put them in bondage to not live life to the fullest. To be full of doubt, sadness, guilt and anger. I have been there and I understand how easy it can be to slip back into bondage. It is my prayer that my fellow Rett parents can break away from the bondage and the lies and trust in God! Open up to truth, find peace and begin to live a life for God as you are called and not let the enemy hold you down!

It would also be ideal, for you to hear our story, to see that we all have struggles, we all have pain. I understand that Rett Syndrome is not the only nasty disease present in this fallen world. Anything from cancer to addiction to traumatic injuries can be just as devastating to live with for yourself or someone you love. The fact of the matter is, we all are experiencing some sort of tragedy in our lives. My families is just a little more obvious as we all parade behind Jocelyn's wheelchair everywhere we go. My prayer for you, after hearing our story, is to find peace that you are not alone in your suffering! I hope that you will be inspired to find trust in God, that He will make good from whatever adversity you are facing. I hope that you will also find a way to break free from the bondage and the lies that are holding you back because of your troubles. And last but not least, I pray you do not live in fear and that you will be willing to share your story when God encourages you to. Don't be afraid of being judged- someone might be going through the same thing you have gone through and if they see you survived it, it will give them hope to stay positive and continue to trust that they too, will survive.

Those would be my ideas as to why God had me write all of this down and share. However, this wasn't my idea in the first place and I could be

100% wrong. And that's okay. Whatever God intends to use this for, He will. I have no expectations. I only want to be obedient to Him and live my life for Him.

"Trust in the Lord with all your heart, and do not lean on your own understanding. In all your ways acknowledge Him, and He will make straight your paths" (Proverbs 3:5-6).

"He said to me, 'My grace is sufficient for you, for my power is made perfect in weakness.' Therefore I will boast all the more gladly of my weaknesses, so that the power of Christ may rest upon me" (2 Corinthians 12:9).

This is all for His glory, not mine…

# Appendix A:
# Jocelyn's Journey Members

*Jocelyn's Journey Board of Directors*
AB & Robi Brand
Bary & Tammy Brand
Kristin Davies
Lori Dechant
Sweta Dedania
Ryan & Crystal Esquivel
Colt & Crystal Gaxiola
Gwen Gollmyer
Dennis & Elizabeth Jones.
John & Jamie Laurent
Eric & Laura Monson
William & Amy Roberts
Robin Taylor
Guy & Heather Thomas
Michael & Heidi Warren
Scott & Katy Webb
Derrick & Amy Wyatt
*Jocelyn's Journey Committee, past and present*
Brenda Bates
Jason & Amy Bates
Meagan Bathurst
Lee & Kristen Cabrera
Ryan Hiatt
Carl & Sally Jones

Kelly Jones

Devon Lazo

Jen Long

Jose & Reana Martinez

Darlene Marquez

Laura Mercado

Marissa Ramos

Jonny & Darby Reece

Sharice Ries

Gerry & Rosie Stringfellow

*Jocelyn's Journey Junior Committee*

Jason Bates, Jr

Emma Cuervo-Davies

Mckenzie & Gavin Esquivel

Jocelyn, Rylee, & Abigail Jones

Jake, Erica, Addisyn, & Andrew Laurent

Caden Mather

Kingston & Austin Monson

Ailish Rasch

London Reedy

Grace Roberts

Vohn & Presley Taylor

Ella, Jack & Ruby Thomas

Noah & Hannah Warren

Nolan, Bodie, & Carson Webb

Aiden & Adalyn Wyatt

# Appendix B: Jocelyn's Journey
## Speeches, unedited, unfiltered

2011

YouTube links to this year's vides:
https://youtu.be/FJBivgSHLa0
https://youtu.be/_TVvopjy-tA

Our speech:
Good evening. My name is Beth and this is my husband Dennis. We are Jocelyn's parents. We wanted to first thank the hard work of our committee and volunteers for getting us here tonight. We would like to thank each and every one of you for your support in coming tonight. Your generous donations during these economic times speaks volumes. Our family is in debt to you for your kindness and love.

Rett Syndrome is considered an "orphan" disease in that it is not very common, only 1 in 10,000 births. It is also important to us to spread awareness as it is to fund research for a cure. Most in the rett community believe rett syndrome is more prevalent than what is documented. With misdiagnoses, some girls go labeled with cerebral palsy, autism, or something else. Imagine those families WHEN there is a cure, their undiagnosed rett daughter goes without treatment. That breaks my heart. Feel free to ask myself, Dennis, or anyone close to Jocelyn if you have any questions about rett. We are all open to talk about it.

When Jocelyn was going through her regression, the best analogy I can give you is when an elderly person is having a stroke. I've never experienced having a loved one suffer from a stroke, but being an ER nurse, I've seen it several times. The devastated family explaining to me "I was just at his house last night, he was fine". More heart wrenching is the patient. Able to obey some commands "squeeze my hands" but can only answer questions as a mumble. Desperately trying to get words out but cannot. Mumbling louder and louder trying to get me to understand what he is saying as tears roll down his face. Finally the frustrated patient gives up and lays quietly in a body that he no longer has control of. The families questions "Will he recover? Will he be the same? Will he ever walk again? Will he ever talk again?" All I can answer is "I don't know" and assure that physical, occupational, and speech therapy will be provided to give him the best possible outcome.

Now imagine the scenario of my elderly patient having a stroke to a one year old. Our little girl. She loved baby dolls. She called me "dude". She could devour a watermelon by herself in minutes. At one year, she could do all of that, but then, all of that was taken away over a short period of time. She could no longer hold her dollies, could only mumble sounds and stopped feeding herself. My toddler, like an elderly man having a stroke, was also very confused and frustrated over this body that she now had little control of. My concerns were the same as the family of a stroke victim "She could hold her sippy cup last week" pleading in confusion. "Will she grow out of this, will she ever talk again, will she ever walk...?" During her regression we were looking and looking for a diagnosis or answers. "I don't know" was our answer with a large dose of physical and occupational therapy to "give her the best possible outcome".

Finally on a dark February afternoon, the diagnosis came. It came with a large helping of denial, anger, bargaining, depression... yes, all the phases of grief and loss. Except for acceptance. I am uncertain we have reached "acceptance" or that we ever will. Every day we help Jocelyn fight Rett Syndrome. We fight it with finding ways to help her. We fight her reflux and GI issues with new diets and supplements. We fight her screaming night terrors with kisses and belly rubs. We fight her heat intolerance by keeping our house cool (I don't want to talk about last months Edison bill). We fight her not being able to stand independently with leg braces. We fight to defend her intelligence by educating people that she is cognitive and aware, despite being nonverbal. We fight to keep her dignity by keeping her on a potty schedule. Everything is a fight. She has to fight her body to do what she wants it to and she doesn't always win. Everyday, Dennis and I will fight rett. On bad days, we chalk one up for rett and reassure ourselves that tomorrow will be better. On good days, we chalk one up for the Jones family and pray for another good day tomorrow. The score is neck and neck, but we know, The Jones Family will ultimately win... soon we hope.

Until then, Jocelyn has extensive therapy in home and at preschool to give us ammo to fight off rett. With the help of Jocelyn's Applied Behavioral Analysis team, we know that Jocelyn knows 10 animals, 10 body parts, 3 letters, 2 numbers, and 9 colors. Her favorite color being.....

well why don't I let her tell you...

[VIDEO]

Despite frustration of not having control of her body, and possibly even feelings of envy, Jocelyn overcomes these feelings and keeps a smile on her face. She strives to satisfy us and is smiles and giggles with pride when she accomplishes a difficult task.

Having rett syndrome as a diagnosis is obviously devastating. However, with the current research funded by Rett Syndrome Research Trust, it is exciting. We know the gene responsible for the disease and we know through the work of professor Bird, the disorder is reversible!

RSRT funds a multitude areas of research simultaneously in attempts to find a cure as soon as possible.

RSRT's "risky research" was worthwhile as researchers have found the first genetic modifier gene for rett syndrome. A modifier gene, by definition, is a gene that modifies the effects produced by another gene. Simply put, rett girls with a modifier gene have less severe symptoms than those girls who do not have a modifier gene. RSRT continues to fund the search for more modifier genes.

Another RSRT funded project involves an immunological study where researchers are transplanting healthy bone marrow into mice models of Rett. Preliminary data suggests there is real reason for optimism.

Pharmacological aspects is another possibility for a cure. However, as mentioned in the video, there is a critical funding gap in the current system of drug development referred to as the Valley of Death. The risky research that RSRT funds would never be funded by conservative agencies. Private funding of RSRT will ensure this "risky research" is done so we learn more about the pathophysiology of rett. The sooner this happens, the sooner industries will step in. Thanks to your support tonight, we are "building a bridge" out of the Valley of Death for Jocelyn and other rett girls on their journey to their cure.

Most recently, I learned of another bridge built in the RSRT world- a communication bridge! Three well known researchers in the rett community have come together to collaborate expertise and knowledge in hopes to speed the path to drug development. Comparing notes from different labs, sharing data, brainstorming between rett research experts... it's an exciting time for us!

Rett syndrome has changed our lives, to say the least. It has taught us many things including how to ask for help, and mostly patients. Not just patients with our nonverbal, sometimes frustrated toddler, but patients for her cure. All we can do to ultimately help Jocelyn is ask for your help to continue to support RSRT, then patiently wait......

I promise, that when that day comes, Jocelyn will personally walk up to each of you and say "Thank you"!

## 2012

YouTube videos for year 2:
https://youtu.be/fUY1v-fUUlg
https://youtu.be/NEkqB-80XIA
https://youtu.be/BTZ-6Vs-f2c
https://youtu.be/Qce-KPRPez8

2012 Speech:

Dennis:

Good evening and welcome to Jocelyn's Journey 2012. Beth and I would first like to thank you all for coming and especially thank you for helping us say good night to Jocelyn in a most memorable way. That was very special and we couldn't have done it without your help.

As mentioned in the video we constantly strive to keep Jocelyn age appropriate. Earlier this year we learned from Jocelyn's peers (or "experts") that the coolest movie out was TANGLED. With that in mind, we played it for background noise during therapy, cooking dinner, cleaning up from dinner... it seemed to be the only movie Jocelyn would sit and watch and giggle. We were proud that she was "cool", liking what was in, but when Beth and I sat and really watched the movie with Jocelyn, we realized why she liked it so much.

Jocelyn views TANGLED as an analogy to her own life. She empathizes with Repunzle because she too was ripped away from her loving parents when she was just a baby. As Repunzle is locked away in a tower, trapped far away from the world, Jocelyn is locked in her body. Both trapped princesses spend most their days only dreaming what it will be like when they finally are free.

This being Jocelyn's TANGLED analogy, tonight would represent the floating lantern scene. A caring community gathers to grieve the loss of the lost princess, but they all release a flying lantern in hopes that one day she will return. Beth and I humbly thank you for coming tonight to help us get our lost princess back.

Beth:

just to clarify the TANGLED analogy, I am not the evil "MOTHER GOTHLE". Just so we are clear. And I'm sorry but the pub scene can't occur until the after party, wherever that may be.

Dennis and I have learned that things could always be worse, and things can always get worse. We are fortunate to have had Jocelyn in the world we live in today. It is a much different world than when Dennis and I were born. Not just because TANGLED is the latest hit, but for many reasons. For example, it was only in the 70's that most "disabled" children were not aloud to go to school. With this segregation came uneducated beliefs and opinions by "typical" kids and their parents. I cannot imagine what it was like for any "special" kids or parents during this period of history. Dennis and I are fortunate that we are special parents in todays world.

Today's world brings us things like our chefs and servers tonight. It is now "cool" to help a child in need rather than segregate them. High school kids, the "teenage years"... what is supposed to be the most selfish time of ones life, these kids are sacrificing their Saturday night, working their butts off, all for our daughter. It is a breathtaking experience to witness these eager young adults striving to help others. For this, we applaud them........... but with that, I also applaud their parents and every person in here who is a parent. Empowering your children to help others and to be accepting of people with a disability or "being different" is changing the world.

Today's technology has also tremendously helped us in raising a rett child. We have made many friends in the rett community on facebook and it is support at the drop of a post. We have made rett family friends from all over the US, the United Kingdom and even Australia. Facebook has been a God send. But facebook has not only brought us friends in the rett community, but also right here in our hometown. Facebook friends who are here tonight, I thank you for your continued support.

Dennis:

In the movie TANGLED, Repunzle had to sing a special song for her magic hair to work it's power. So I will now sing you that song so rett will be cured and we get our Princess Jo Jo back................. just kidding, I'll let Repunzle do the singing!

[video]

### *Science*

Beth:

Dennis and I know we cannot "make the clock reverse" but science has shown we can "save what has been lost"!

This past March as I was plotting my revenge on Rett Syndrome by planning this very evening, I noticed a new post on facebook on the RSRT page. A wonderfully presented ten minute presentation of how the immune system is thought to have a play in rett and it's horrid symptoms. A finding that a research lab, funded by RSRT, discovered. The presentation further explained how bone marrow transplants have shown to be effective and RSRT currently has the goal to launch a clinical trial as quickly as possible. I re-lived an overwhelming since of appreciation to our donators who helped us raise $53,000 at last year's "Jocelyn's Journey" for RSRT. Your support last year contributed to this study and now has RSRT posting things such as "The goal is to launch a clinical trial as quickly as possible".

Being an RN, I understand the risk of chemo, radiation, and a bone marrow transplant. On the other hand, I understand the benefit of our daughter no longer having Rett Syndrome. I still felt I needed Jocelyn's consent or permission to accept this treatment, if in fact it follows through.

The next night I as I snuggled and rocked her before bed I explained: "Jo, the doctors might have found a medicine to help you walk, talk, play, not have tummy aches..."

She replied "giggle, giggle giggle"

I further explained: "The medicine might make you very sick for a long time. You will be in a room with only Mommy or Daddy for a little while. No school. No friends. And it might hurt."

She leaned into me, looked me in the eye with a clumsy stiff arm flung on my shoulder, to ensure she had my attention. She replied looking deeply at me: "eeeyyeeee, eyyyeee, eyyyye, eyyyyeee...."

I was still unsure if she understood. I continued: "This medicine isn't for sure that it will work, but it worked in animals and they can now walk and play after getting the medicine."

Jo replied: "giggle giggle giggle"

I asked again: "Do you want Mommy & Daddy to try the medicine for you, even if it hurts and makes you sick?"

With another stiff arm on my shoulder, serious look on her face and deep eye contact, she consented : "eyyyyeee, eyyyyeee, eyyyyeee..... giggle giggle giggle". Just another verification that our child is well aware of what is going on around her and what is to be expected.

We have accepted her consent to go through with a clinical trial of a chemo or radiation with a bone marrow transplant, when and if invited to do so. Again, I am reminded of our analogy of Tangled with Jocelyn's life: Repunzle had to loose her hair to break free, and so may Jocelyn...

In the mean time we wait, and fundraise, and hope to learn that this year's "Jocelyn's Journey" event will not just go towards researching for a cure, but go towards funds for Jocelyn's clinical trial for treatment.

Dennis:

Meanwhile, RSRT does not put all it's eggs in one basket. There are still hopeful studies being conducted such as deep brain stimulation (which is also being used for Parkinson's, depression and other disorders). There are also RSRT funded research labs dealing with gene therapy which are also showing signs of success. RSRT is also supporting a project looking for mutations in other genes which counter the damage caused by the mutated Rett gene. This study is described as "intriguing" by RSRT and they are learning there are some drugs that already exist that may help in this particular study.

Though research is currently very promising and exciting, we are still dealing with Rett on a daily basis. We take care of Jocelyn to the best of our abilities and have numerous doctor's appointments, meetings with schools and therapists... every time we encounter someone who is unfamiliar with Jo or Rett, we have to explain all over again:

she cannot walk, talk or use her hands.
she cannot blow a bubble.
she cannot feed herself or hold my hand.
she cannot ride a bike or play soccer.
cannot tell us what hurts or say "I love you".
there is so much she cannot do.

But what supersedes all of the "CANNOTS" is what our daughter CAN DO! Take a look around the room. Our daughter can gather over 300 people in a room to raise money to save lives, and help change the world!

THAT IS WHAT OUR DAUGHTER CAN DO!

**2013**

YouTube videos from the Brave year:
https://youtu.be/-Fwh0YL7JDI
https://youtu.be/MJdLoueUsYg

Speech outline for the Brave year:
Rock the mic

* Brave committee
* Brave Husband
* Bravest is Jo starting at 1 year old! regression, I was in the closet 6 weeks pregnamt
* Our year of being "Brave" started before Jo Journey 2012. as a ff and RN, still, seeing your child not breath for any length of time is too long.
* Kindergarten, IEP's= great team, all trying to do what's best for Jo.
* G-tube: decided in March, Scheduled April 15.
   * - April 12th I learned about 2 Rett girls
   * general anesthesia... neurological disorder...
   * - we were late, dropped us off
   * - finally in a full WR with Jo...

# MOVIE

* A pictures says 1000 words.
* She is doing extremely well and gets plenty of water and the nutrition that she needs.
* I share this part of Jocelyn's Journey with you because this is what made the journey a game changer.
* We were terrified, but what scared me more was regretting not doing it.
* We faced our fears and we learned, what is on the other side of fear was well worth the whole experience. Because of Jocelyn and this moment of our journey, our FAITH is stronger than our FEAR!
* It isn't easy getting up in front of over 200 people and expose my family every year, telling stories like this. but I recently read in a book :
    * - "To remain comfortable is to help yourself. To get uncomfortable, you will help others".

* Shortly after her surgery, I brought the girls to the gym with me:
    * - Does she walk? talk? why? why rett?
    * day 2
    * day 3
    * a week went by before I realized: the message wasn't for him, the message was for me!

* Blessed to have RSRT
    * - 97% of every dollar
    * - the morals to share research so other diseases can have an expedited cure
    * - we have clinical trials and have cured mice...
    * - WE ARE SO CLOSE!
    * - Just as I need O2 in my lungs to live, RSRT needs funding for a cure to come so PLEASE, be BRAVE during the auction that is about to take place.

- ★ Most parents would empathize with me with the feeling of "there has to be something else more I can do to help my child"
  - ★ So I am getting uncomfortable by sharing this story because it is WHY JOCELYN HAS RETT SYNDROME!
  - ★ To teach "US" to take care of each other and LOVE each other, no matter what!
  - ★ Not just physically, not just the sick... but whatever/whoever is in YOUR life. GO TAKE CARE OF THEM AND LOVE THEM NO MATTER WHAT!
  - ★ RSRT having money is fueling a cure, but LOVE could expedite it.

- ★ My 5 year old is extremely powerful and inspiring- if you allow her to be.
  - ★ - she can't walk, she can't talk, but she has forever changed the way I live my life. LET HER INSPIRE YOU TO DO THE SAME.

- ★ In the next few days, my mom will call me with the total raised for this year's event and I will excitedly pass that on to all of you. It is a very fun celebration and everyone gets excited and it feels amazing to be directly contributing to Jocelyn's cure!
- ★ With funding, what if throughout the year, we continue to support the journey by helping us fulfill Jocelyn's purpose: TO TAKE CARE OF EACH OTHER AND LOVE EACH OTHER NO MATTER WHAT!
- ★ Once you are BRAVE enough to get uncomfortable, face a fear (rather it be a conversation you've been avoiding, a DECISION, whatever...) Jocelyn would LOVE to hear about how she inspired you to do that, and she would LOVE to hear how wonderful you feel, after facing that fear.
- ★ I am only the voice used to fulfill Jocelyn's purpose: TO TEACH US TO TAKE CARE OF EACH OTHER AND LOVE EACH OTHER NO MATTER WHAT! If we follow this golden rule, I know the cure for Rett syndrome will be expedited.

**2014**

YouTube videos:
https://youtu.be/zguqpCXuSQY
https://youtu.be/iMGCvlhgIDY

2014 speech

Thank you so much, everyone for joining us here tonight. Dennis and I are so appreciative of your support. Tonight I'd like to share a little about where we've been and where we're going.

I'm a "tough love" kind of parent. For example, once Jocelyn was able to do things on her own, that was it! Do it again. Let's go! Moving forward! Check! Check! Next milestone! As soon as she was on solids, I would make that little muffin gourmet breakfast every day! eggs, french toast, freshly cut fruit in the morning, sandwiches, spaghetti, chicken, sweet potatoes, squash for lunch and dinner... THAT GIRL WOULD GRUB DOWN! Cleared her plate! Sure it was in her hair, on the floor... it was awesome! "MMMM, yummm, nummm nummm" she would say as she ate!

But right after her first birthday, she started to just stare at her breakfast. I was annoyed how she kept putting her hands in her mouth. The dentist said she was teething, but this was ridiculous! Soon, She would cry at breakfast now! My "nummm mmmm nummm" girl turned into a defiant terror- I thought. Welp, I knew she could feed herself, she's done it for months now, and I refused to baby her and hand feed her. This was ridiculous! I would get so mad at Dennis when he would "give in to her" and spoon feed her. "You're spoiling her" I would tell him.

But then it wasn't just breakfast she wouldn't eat. Then it was lunch too. She would cry and cry and cry and put her hands in her mouth. I refused to give in! Early terrible 2's or something! Maybe she's mad she can't crawl or walk yet. At one point my mom pointed out she stopped saying "mom" and "dog" and "dada" and "hi". "Yes, she still does!" I argued. Looking back now I think I was so concerned with her not eating that I hadn't noticed she didn't called for me much anymore. I needed her to eat! That would fix things! Nutrition is so important, especially the first 5 years. That's what all the books say. She needs energy! To gain some weight!

One day, enough was enough. I got upset. I got her out of her high chair from her second meal of the day I prepared, that she didn't eat. I took her to my bedroom and I stood her up supported by my bed and sat down in front of her- eye to eye. I begged her "STOP IT JOCELYN! WHY WONT YOU EAT! YOU HAVE TO EAT! STOP PUTTING YOUR HANDS IN YOUR MOUTH! YOUR TEETH ARE FINE! EVERYBODY GROWS TEETH!"

Jocelyn started to get her precious lip out! My begging turned into a bawling blubbering cry: "WHAT'S WRONG WITH YOU? YOU WONT EVEN TRY!" At that moment, Jocelyn began to cry and vigorously shook her head "NO NO NO NO" as if she were telling me: "you've got it all wrong, Mom, STOP!" At that moment, I stopped crying and I was so proud that she communicated. She told me "NO!" I got through to her, but more importantly, SHE got through to ME! I could see it in her eyes-the last thing she wanted to do was disappoint me. I wiped my tears and hers, swallowed my pride, made her another lunch and spoon fed it to her- AND SHE ATE IT! This was the moment my quest began. Something beyond my daughter's control was overcoming her- and it infuriated me! I was no longer "tough loving" her- I then knew, she wanted help! She was trying to figure out too, what was wrong. Her "NO NO NO" of her head vigorously shaking was my wake up call and her desperate cry for help. This was no longer "her against me". I was in this with her and I was going to love her through it and be there every heart beat of the way!

I strived to come up with the best analogy for you, what the emotional journey felt like. I'm sure most of you have been in Target, Albertsons or some sort of store when your toddler conveniently wonders off. At first you are sure to find them. "Jocelyn... Jocelyn..." then a little bit of annoyance sets in: " Jocelynnnn. knock it off" you may have threatened. Then, after a few moments pass, the slightest sign of panic "Jocelyn!" you demand "Jocelyn!" and you start searching isle after isle. Still too proud to ask for help "Jocelyn! Jo! Jo! Jocelyn JOCELYN!" No hope- you can't find her! By now, you figure, she is getting further and further away from you. Time to act quickly- Finally- in an act of desperation you ask a stranger for help, then another, then another...: "My daughter- she's lost! This is what happened... Can you help me? My daughter- she's lost! This is what happened... Can you help me? My daughter- she is lost..." you explain in great, sometimes embarrassing, detail of every event that took place, leading up to the drifting away- this is what it was like in the 9 different specialists multiple diagnostic studies we went visited in the beginning of our journey, over and over and over and over. "normal pregnancy, full term cecearian due to desells, no drinking no drugs, no family history..."

During your search in the store for any sign of your child, you occasionally notice another person with just as much desperation on their faces. A little bit of curiosity sets in: what was their story? what or who did they loose? what were desperately seeking to find or hold onto. The curiosity quickly passes though- I'm on a mission- I have to find Jo!

Suddenly- a positive sign arrises in the store- you find your child's toy! It marks the beginning of a trail towards finding her- towards getting her back! This is how it felt when we got our diagnosis- "SHE'S THIS WAY!" you'd yell in the store. Suddenly, another toy of her's you find: We found RSRT and the exciting research: we have a gene! A mouse model that proves this is reversible! There is hope!

Now is the time to act even more quickly- time for a search party. There is no way Dennis and I could find Jocelyn on our own- we need help! We called out to friends, family, the community... "Jocelyn's Journey", all of you... our search party. We cover so much more ground and it has expedited finding Jocelyn so much! In the sometimes frantic search of looking and looking and gathering more search party members to help us- it is so difficult for Dennis and I to express how much it means to us that you- YOU all are on this search with us. We could not have come this far without the communities continued support. We couldn't cover as much ground without each and every one of you, as well as all the businesses who support by donating gifts for the evening. Everyone pitching in- doing and giving what they can to help us. It is a very humbling feeling that Dennis and I and will forever be grateful for.

But the search is not over- it is not time to rest, it is time to move quickly! More hope is all around us with the gene consortium that RSRT has put together, we have Dr Ali right in our own back yard with his projects that will dramatically change Jocelyn's life. It is time to press on- OKAY SEARCH PARTY! You all got your maps tonight, you got your satchel on you chair- Let's go! She is just around the corner- we are so close!

But before we press on- I must share with you: What we will find when we do get to Jocelyn back- we are also going to find something bigger than you could imagine… Check it out!

VIDEO

In store, when we find Jocelyn, maybe hidden in the clothes racks- we are going to find thousands of girls sitting right next to her. Jocelyn's Journey isn't just about Jocelyn- it's about Lani, Amanda, Emma, Elenore, Chelsea… and so many more.

Then, remember the other panicked parents we saw in the store that we were curious about? They are going to see us, finding our girls and be filled with HOPE!

Ladies and gentleman, I present to you the leaders of the search party: the Jocelyn's Journey Committee.

When we gathered in January, I asked the committee: what's next? We are going to find Jocelyn soon, but then what? Do we all chest bump and all go to the river and go about our lives? We all agreed and committed: NO! We keep going with Jocelyn's Journey! We want to help the other parents in the store- who needed help finding their loved one- just like Dennis and I did. What would we be teaching our children if we get what we want then quit- No, we must help others and teach them what we've learned, and show them what we did, on our search party to find Jocelyn. Curing Jocelyn not only gets the committee another envelope stuffing member, but it also sets the precedence of what we can do! What this community can do.

For starters- I cannot begin to tell you how many times Jocelyn was almost mis-diagnosed in the beginning. If that were to happen, we wouldn't have found RSRT. There is such a broad spectrum of Rett symptoms that I know there are girls out there misdiagnosed and it nauseates me! We are going to have a cure and they will be sitting in wheelchairs, speechless and cognitive with no hope. I asked Monica Coenrads- executive director of RSRT, what was next for her- once we cure Rett Syndrome, what will she then do? She said she will be on a quest to find such girls to get them treatment and their cure. And now, Jocelyn's Journey committee would like to recognize you, and our top contributors to the search party:

Golden Gate Bridge Sponsors: AB and GG
Coronado Bridge Sponsor: Brenda Bates
Tower Bridge Sponsors: San Bernardino County Fire Fighters, Local 935
        Carl & Sally Jones
        London Bridge Sponsors: Kevin & Allison Foley
        American Solar Direct
        Derrick & Amy Wyatt
        San Bernardino County Fire Fighters Assoication
        AdvoCare- Jahmal & Serina Williams
        Ripley & Associates
        Interstate Concrete Cutting WITH HOD
        Carriers and Laborers, Local #783
Brookly Bridge Sponsors: The Dechant Family
        Gary & Lynn Miyata
        Advocare, Sharice Ries
        Ft Irwin Fire
        Noteworthy Promotions

Mojave Bridge Sponsors:   Ryan & Kristina Vanderpool
        Jim & Andrea
        Kory & Jennifer
        Leo & Georgette Jodoin
        Frank & Freda Dalla Valle
        James & Missy Guffy

Pedestrian Bridge Spnosors: Valley-HI Honda
Last, but not least, we'd like to recognize our Master of Ceremonies for 4 years in a row now: Cliff Earp!

Please know that Jocelyn's Journey is not just a one night event- we live this year round- inviting everyone and anyone to help us on the search. Tonight, if it is in your heart to help us in a year round effort and you'd like to join the committee, please talk to one of us tonight or in the near future. e-mail us at information@jocelynsjourney.org or send us a message on Facebook.

Even if you aren't on the committee, you can still help us make Jocelyn's Journey a year long event. Please, go into the community and share our story! And support our supporters. If you need:

Solar panels: talk to my friend Shawn at American Solar Direct
Something demolished, talk to my brother or Junior at Interstate Concrete Cutting
If you want to be a Champion, talk to and AdvoCare's Sharice or Jahmal
If your house is on fire: call SB county association or the union... or try calling Ft. Irwin fire... j/k
call Dennis!

One last request before we start some prizes- when you go home tonight, please tell your children where you were tonight- what you are a part of! You are playing a HUGE part in saving so many lives! Your children are watching you and will do what you do. One of our committee members was collecting gift cards from local businesses for tonight's event. Her daughter, who is only 2 months younger than Jocelyn, was watching her and asked "mommy, is that for Jocelyn?"

"Yes" she answered. The little girl ran to her room and when she came out she handed her mom 2 build a bear gift cards and said "Could you use these for her too, please?"

Thank you everyone and have a wonderful evening!

**2015**

Dennis:
Good evening and welcome to the 5th annual Jocelyn's Journey Gala. For those of you who don't know me, my name is Dennis and I'm Jocelyn's dad. I'd like to thank you all for sharing this special evening with us.

I sure am happy that my wife FINALLY gave me the mic this year!

She tends to be a mic hog! That is actually a joke as I don't like being in the spotlight at all! EVER! But I'll do it for Jocelyn. There isn't much a father wouldn't do for his little girl.

It's hard to believe this is our 5th Gala. I'd be lying if I told you this event was easy. It can be overwhelming at times for my wife and the committee. I've always said it's like planning a wedding, every year, on a zero budget. And they do it! And they do a great job. Myself and the committee know, this event wouldn't be what it is without you, our guests, sitting in those seats year after year. There aren't words to express how grateful we are for your support.

My "Pretty Girl" Jocelyn is so lovable, silly and most of the time happy. However on days she struggles with Rett, she is left frustrated and almost seems lonely in this world. One of the worst things of having a child with Rett is knowing Jocelyn cannot do what "typical" kids her age can do. She cannot tell me what's wrong, what hurts... she cannot ask for more cake or a piece of candy... she cannot run or throw a ball... As a father, this kills me that I cannot immediately fix the problem at hand. I'm the dad, the man, the head of house... I'm supposed to fix things, be the problem solver. When I can't I feel like I'm letting her down.

Jocelyn's Journey alleviates that pain of not being able to immediately fix things for Jocelyn. We are doing our part to get her cured, which be the ultimate "fix". Without your support and attendance year after year, this could not be possible. From the bottom of my heart, Beth and I, and the Jocelyn's Journey committee, thank you!


Beth:


Hello and good evening. Thank you for once again, helping us fund a cure for Rett Syndrome.

I cannot believe this is our 5th Jocelyn's Journey Gala. There are many of you who have been here every single year and Dennis and I are humbled for your generous, continuous support. There are also many of you here tonight for the first time. Again, Dennis and I are extremely grateful for your support and hope you are enjoying yourself tonight and hope that you will make this an annual "date night" with us.

YEAR 5!!! I wanted something special for this big mile stone.

When researching "5 year anniversary" ideas, I found the Rose Quartz. According to some, the Rose Quartz is the 5 year anniversary gemstone.

The more I researched the meaning of this gemstone, the more fitting it was for our event.

It is described as "a stone of the heart"- a crystal of **UNCONDITIONAL LOVE.** How appropriate for our family, and any family with a Rett or special needs child. "Unconditional love" is defined as love without limitations or conditions. Dennis and I are a part of a "club" who no one ever willingly signs up for. It's a club of every parents biggest fear. It's a club that is so undesirable, some choose not to be parents at all. It's the club of "special parents". A club of "I have a sick child". A club of "things didn't turn out the way I envisioned". As a group, we helplessly watch our children suffer, hurt, and and exist in life, not as children are intended to.

While the term "unconditional love" is appropriate for Dennis and I loving our daughter, despite her limitations, it is also appropriate for Jocelyn's love for us. Despite our extreme efforts to give Jocelyn a typical childhood, because of Rett, we fail her every day. Jocelyn graciously forgives us without a second thought and loves us unconditionally with her daily snuggles and infectious laughter.

The unconditional love is also felt by you, our yearly guests for Jocelyn's Journey. We do not deserve your kindness and support, yet you all show up year after year, donating to help us cure our daughter. Dennis and I are forever in debt for your generosity, support, and unconditional love!

Rose Quartz is said to also have healing properties that is believed to help let go of **anger, resentment** and **jealousy** while encouraging **forgiveness**. These are all very powerful words!

Anger and resentment are a given "normal" for everyone in the "special parent" club. It's part of grieving. Angry that things didn't turn out the way we envisioned. Angry our child has to suffer. Angry that we cannot immediately fix any problem at hand.

Jealousy- This is a huge one for me that I still struggle with to this day. As I scroll through my Facebook feed and see women I was pregnant with in 2008, signing up their 7 year old for soccer, talking about what funny thing their child had to say that day, or even complain at the mischief they got into… my stomach immediately turns with nauseating envy.

But worse than that, when we are at birthday parties, BBQs or family gatherings and all the kids are running around screaming, laughing, and playing with each other as sweet Jocelyn sits by me in her wheelchair watching from afar- that absolutely KILLS me! I can only imagine her level of jealousy for the other children. I do what I can to have her be included, and most kids are receptive, but it just isn't the same. Having the freedom to not be attached to Dennis or I 24/7 is something we dream about with Jocelyn.

Forgiveness- Forgiveness is huge in our home. Jocelyn forgives us at our short comings daily. Dennis and I have to constantly forgive each other for the same. The added stress of having a special child in the family cannot be described and to truly understand, one would have to experience it. Every aspect of our life is effected and no one in our house is perfect, so forgiveness is a daily activity for survival.

In the past, some of you may have witnessed a moment of anger expressed by Dennis and I on a bad day on our journey, forgive us.

If Jocelyn is having a bad day and we are in public and she is throwing a fit, please, forgive us.

A lot of you in this room are the families on my Facebook feed, with healthy children whom we are envious of, please, forgive us.

And last but not least, it is impossible for Dennis and I to express just how grateful we are for each and every one of you for your continuos support, please forgive us.

Now, I know that a gemstone wont cure Rett. But the Rose Quartz's meaning had a lot of significance for this year, obviously. And how appropriate that it's PINK! I thought it'd be perfect for Dennis, make him feel more at home, being surroundded by so much PINK! For those of you who don't know, 6 weeks ago, Dennis and I had our THIRD girl! Poor Dennis!

Having a Rett child can be difficult, being pregnant and having a Rett Child is downright HARD! Dennis and I just kept reassuring ourselves, "Enjoy it, it's our last time".

When Abbie was born, and she was so tiny and cute and perfect, again, we told ourselves "Enjoy it, it's our last time".

When she outgrew her newborn clothes at one month old and we remembered just how fast babies grow, we strive not to be sad, but just to "Enjoy it, it's our last time".

We will continue with this attitude with Abbie, her first babble, first words, first time she feeds herself, first steps... we will enjoy every second of it and soak it up because we know, this is our last experiences of firsts.

A few weeks ago, however, I realized something exciting: it's NOT our last time! NO, I'm not pregnant- that's not funny! The exciting thing is that we get to experience Jocelyn's firsts AGAIN. I know, I will hear the **first** time Jocelyn calls me "Mama" **again**. We will watch the **first** time Jocelyn feeds herself **again**. How exciting, for everyone, the **first** time we watch Jocelyn manipulate a toy appropriately **again**. Jocelyn had many "firsts" when she was a baby, but most of them before she was two. Dennis and I work to fund her cure with Jocelyn's Journey, and we wait patiently for it to come and experience all of Jocelyn's "**first again's**".

However, there is one matter that Dennis and I would gladly have be our LAST TIME! The matter of making big decisions for our daughter to fight back the physical effects Rett Syndrome has left her with. The last time we had to make a big decision was 2 years ago when Jocelyn had a feeding tube surgically put in place. It was a very scary time for us, but Jocelyn did great with the surgery and has thrived with the supplemental feeds. This time, we are faced with the decision of spinal surgery. Not one, but 2 rods will be put in our 40 pound 7 year old within the next 6 months, to correct her scoliosis. Scoliosis is common in Rett and you can see in the pictures in the movie we just played for you, just how bad Jocelyn's is. As if our girls didn't struggle enough, Rett is very taxing on our girl's bodies.

Dennis and I are hoping and praying for this one to be our LAST TIME:
The last time
we sign consent for our daughter to get cut.
The last time
we have to explain a procedure to Jocelyn and hope she doesn't have any unanswered questions
The last time
Jocelyn has to be "nothing by mouth" after midnight
The last time

we leave our other children behind while we stay with Jocelyn in the hospital

It infuriates me what we face as a family and it kills me to think of what Jocelyn must overcome on a daily basis, let alone when something big like this comes along. There is nothing more frustrating, as a parent, than to not be able to fix a problem your child is dealing with. First and for most, I pray. Next, I turn that anger into energy towards Jocelyn's Journey!

I can't correct my daughter's wavy spine, but I can put together a nice raffle basket.

I can't swallow for my daughter, but I can talk to a stranger about Rett Syndrome and how we will cure it.

I can't read my daughter's thoughts and answer every question she may have, but I can invite invite invite someone to help us, but funding her cure!

God willing, this will be the last time, Rett strikes us and wins a battle by taking her spine. But soon, because of RSRT and generous contributors like yourselves, we will win the WAR and we will get our Baby Jo back and witness all of her "first agains"!

Printed in the United States
By Bookmasters